THE OTHER BRANDS OF

A COMPLETE GUIDE BY PAUL FOX

ISBN: 978-1-57424-271-3
SAN 683-8022

P.O. Box 17878 – Anaheim Hills, CA 92817

Acknowledgements

Mike Newton for his countless contributions to this book. Rod McDonald for his generosity in sharing his collection of Gibson and Kalamazoo ephemera. Mark at Folkway Music for the use of so many great photos. Steve at Elderly Instruments for tracking down many great photos of rare instruments. Arian Sheets and the National Music Museum. Tony Klassen, John Thomas, Deke Dickerson, Turtlehill Banjos, Roy Book Binder, Neil Reck, Joe Spann, and Ron Middlebrook a fantastic publisher.

This book is dedicated to my amazing wife.

Table of Contents

The Origin of the Gibson-made Brands

In order to provide some context around the development of Gibson's other brands, let's start in the early 1920's when Gibson's management team consisted of Lewis A. Williams as general manager, C.V. Buttelman, Sales & Marketing Manager, Ted McHugh, Chief Engineer and Lloyd Loar, Acoustical Engineer. Other than the head of Gibson's board, Judge John Adams, these were the men who had been running the company for many years. Gibson was making an attempt to resurrect the waning popularity of the mandolin and was expending a lot of resources to develop the master series Style 5 instruments, which included the F5 mandolin, L5 guitar, H5 mandola, and K5 mando-cello. Williams was investing heavily in the development of the Model F-5, as the cornerstone of the mandolin's resurgence he hoped would bring Gibson to new heights. The F5 is the most replicated mandolin design of all time, but would prove to be the downfall of the management team and Williams in particular, who was banking on the mandolin making a big comeback. As it turned out, he was wrong. The company was near bankruptcy as competitors like Epiphone, Bacon & Day and Lange/Paramount were years ahead of Gibson manufacturing banjos for the latest craze in music, Jazz. The banjo had become the preferred fretted instrument for early Jazz, and the mandolin was quickly becoming obsolete. Williams, Loar and Buttelman all wound up leaving Gibson by 1924, making way for a new management team.

The origins of Gibson's other brands should be divided into two separate eras. The first, 1929 to 1932 was a direct result of the efforts by Gibson's sales and marketing manager, Frank Campbell. It was in January of 1925, Gibson's new General Manager, Guy Hart named Frank Campbell as the new head of sales and advertising. Campbell was the perfect man for the job having worked for Gibson in field sales, service and had substantial experience in musical merchandizing and retail. His background also included working at the Grinnell Brothers store in Detroit, MI, one of Gibson's largest distributors, and had returned to Gibson in May of 1924 and being promoted to Sales Manager made Frank Campbell the #2 man behind Hart in Gibson's new management team. He spent much of his time traveling all over the U.S., selling and promoting Gibson instruments, setting up new dealers and attending various trade shows and conventions. This was the beginning of a whole new era in the history of Gibson, as they had to remedy the company's sagging sales that had nearly caused their bankruptcy in 1923. Their singular focus was to become more competitive in the exploding banjo market by improving their banjo designs, which paled by comparison to their competitors. Campbell's exceptional sales and advertising skills got things going in a hurry as Gibson reported record sales in 1926 and even a bigger year in 1928. They had developed "The Mastertone" banjo line, entirely new and improved instruments that were not only surpassing their competitors, but also stand as some of the best banjos ever made.

In 1926, Gibson introduced their first official flattop guitars, Models L-1 and L-0, hoping to capitalize on another new fad, Hawaiian guitar music. Designing and building these new guitar designs would have required a collaborative effort between many of Gibson's key employees, including Ted McHugh, still Gibson's Chief Engineer, and inventor of the truss rod and adjustable height bridge; A.C Stout, production manager and Campbell as the "eyes and ears" of Gibson in the field. An October, 1926 issue of Gibson's Mastertone Magazine called Hart, Campbell, and Stout the "three men who are the guiding forces back of Gibson, Inc. These were the men that would fuel some of the most creative and interesting new instrument designs Gibson had seen since the early 1920's.

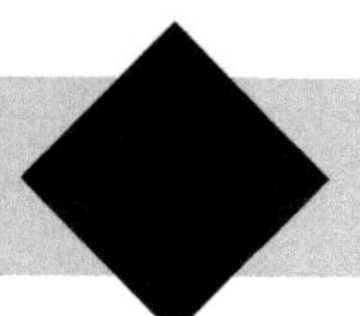

Frank Campbell, Gibson's Sales Manager from 1925 to 1931

All of Gibson's new flattop designs between 1926 and 1932 varied greatly, suggesting a very experimental and transitional period for the Kalamazoo Company. There were multiple body sizes and shapes, 12, 13, and 14-fret necks (number of frets clear of the body), elevated "archtop" style fingerboards, adjustable height bridges with extension tailpieces, various flattop bridge shapes, and much more. Gibson had decided to use the same size body as the previous archtop Model L-1 and L Jr. being 13 ¾" wide at the lower bout. It enabled them to re-use existing tooling including the side bending forms and body molds that were no longer in production. Then in 1929, Gibson introduced a newer, larger body flattop guitar model, the L-2 with a 14 ¾" wide lower bout and 13-fret neck. This design would prove to be the prototype for Gibson's "L" series flattops for the next 15 years, as well as many of their early non-Gibson brands as well. By 1930, all of their flattops inherited this new design, including the legendary Nick Lucas Special, the L-1, and L-0.

The first official non-Gibson brand was the "Oriole" budget banjo, a lower cost tenor banjo that was offered to existing dealers such as J.W. Jenkins in Kansas City, MO. The Oriole name was probably derived from the famed Oriole Orchestra that Gibson had been associated with through their relationship with Nick Lucas, the "Crooning Troubadour". In 1928, Gibson introduced the first-ever "artist-endorsed" guitar with Nick Lucas's name and picture on the label, and Nick was the star of the Oriole orchestra in Chicago. Almost simultaneously, Gibson built the first private-label banjos for the Trujo Banjo Company in San Francisco called the "Truett", named after co-owner Velma Truett. Neither the Oriole or Truett brands lasted very long, but it would not be the end of Gibson's efforts to sell lower cost instruments to those who could not afford the genuine article.

In 1930, Gibson started making the first of its own "in-house" brand of guitars and banjos called Kel Kroydon. By May 1930 Gibson had two Kel Kroydon guitar models, based on their new 14 ¾" body size, and two banjo models as well. Their aim was to produce less expensive versions of their own Gibson-branded instruments by cutting production costs. First, they eliminated their patented truss rod, and built guitars with much lighter weight materials. Gibson would maintain that the patented truss rod was one of the key features that distinguished a Gibson from any of their other brands. In addition, Gibson also started another rather odd enterprise - wooden toy manufacturing and also used the Kel Kroydon name for a line of model sailboats. It was also at this time that Frank Campbell started business relationships with other companies to manufacture these same basic guitars using different name brands. One of the first to capitalize on the Gibson-made instruments was The Montgomery Ward mail-order catalog company, who had Gibson build a guitar using their own brand name - Recording King. The first guitar was nearly the same as the most expensive flattop model Gibson made, The Nick Lucas Special, only finished in all black lacquer. As early as the fall of 1929, Montgomery Ward had also introduced the Gibson-made "Studio King" budget banjo, and the "Recording King" Model 505, which was a very fancy model complete with gold-plated hardware. Campbell also struck up deals with Buegeleisen & Jacobson to make banjos and guitars using the S.S. Stewart brand.

Whether or not these new ventures were a direct result of the beginning of the Great Depression is somewhat unclear. After all, it was only a few short months after the Stock Market Crash of October 1929 when these new projects were begun. With the exception of the Recording King brand, most of the early Gibson-made brands lasted a very short one to two years suggesting that the Great Depression had the opposite effect - making it impossible to continue to produce these smaller quantity, off-brands for very long.

Gibson's Assistant to the General Manager, Neil Abrams

The second era for the Gibson-made brands started after Frank Campbell's departure from Gibson in December 1931, by his successor, Neil Abrams. Abrams' official title was "Assistant to the General Manager" (Guy Hart), but his duties encompassed many different areas of Gibson's operations during the 1930's. For all intents and purposes, Abrams took over the role of sales and marketing manager and helped Gibson launch some very successful brands and establish other relationships with companies like The Tonk Brothers, and large distributors like Continental Music, Grossman's Music, and J.W. Jenkins. This second era saw the introduction Gibson's most successful "budget brand" - Kalamazoo, which would out-sell every other non-Gibson brand they manufactured from 1929 to World War II. Abrams was also part of the development of the Cromwell line, Gibson's second "in-house" brand that was also very successful in terms of units sold. Secondary brands like Old Kraftsman, Fascinator, Hayden, Capital, and Mastertone Special were just a few of the brands Gibson made during Abrams' tenure.

Gibson's work force in the 1930's was over 200 employees and they were able to keep working because of Gibson's willingness to try new things and not solely rely on the Gibson brand to carry the company. While many other instrument manufacturers went out of business during the Great Depression, the "budget brands," helped keep production running at near full capacity. The success of brands like Kalamazoo, Cromwell and Recording King carried the company through very hard economic times, and possibly saved the company all together. Several of the early brands were as few as two guitars, but the post-1932 brands were mostly larger quantities manufactured to sell at very low prices. By 1937, Gibson hit peak production of the off-brands and by 1940 they had produced a total of 31 separate and distinct brands. However, 1940 would see most of the brands disappear and with exception of the Kalamazoo brand and the guitars Gibson made for National Valco, none of the other brands would ever be made again. While most of the 31 brands were only manufactured for fairly short periods of time during the mid-1930's, they would prove to be some of the most interesting and collectable guitars Gibson ever produced.

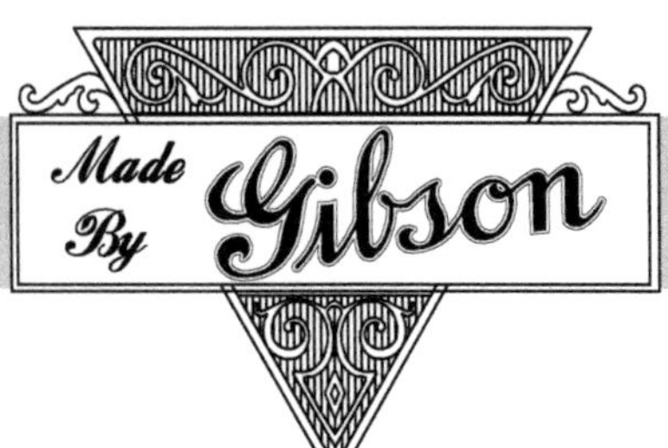

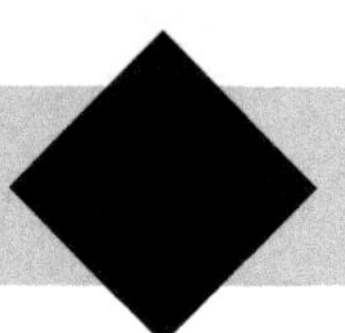

While there is much that is not known about many of the Gibson-made brands, this book takes an in-depth look at all of the known brands Gibson made from 1929 to 1961 including Ambassador, B&S Barrington, Capital, Carson J. Robison, Charles McNeil, Cromwell, Fascinator, FDH, Grinnell, Hayden, Kalamazoo, Kel Kroydon, Liberty, Henry L. Mason, Marshall Special, Martelle, Mastertone Special, Mitchell Brothers, Old Kraftsman (Spiegel), Oriole, Paynes, Recording King & Studio King (Montgomery Ward), Reznick Radio Special, S.S. Stewart, Tex Star, Trujo/Truett, Washburn, and Werlein Leader.

Various Gibson brands price lists and pricing memos from the 1930s.

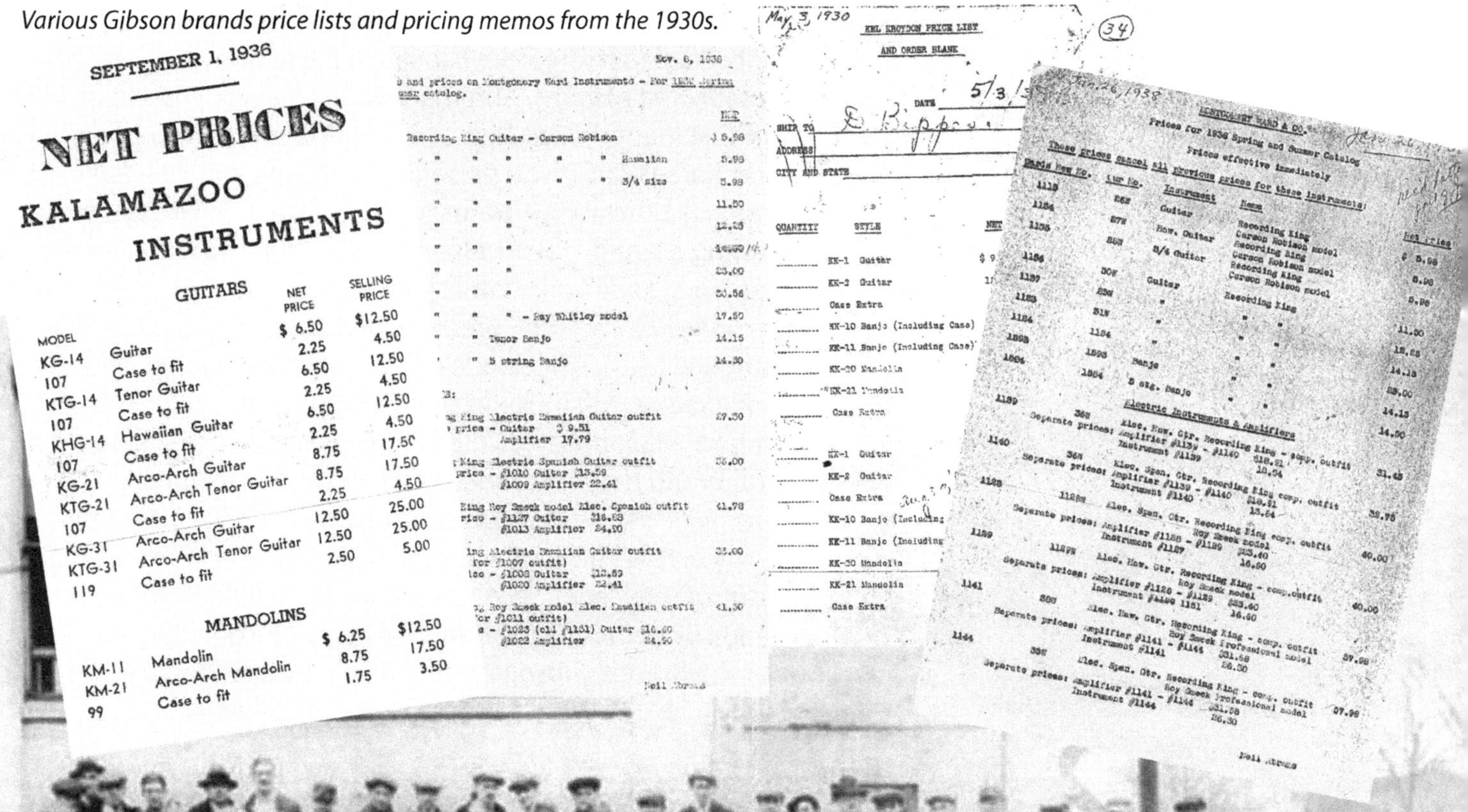

SEPTEMBER 1, 1936

NET PRICES

KALAMAZOO INSTRUMENTS

GUITARS

MODEL		NET PRICE	SELLING PRICE
KG-14	Guitar	$ 6.50	$12.50
107	Case to fit	2.25	4.50
KTG-14	Tenor Guitar	6.50	12.50
107	Case to fit	2.25	4.50
KHG-14	Hawaiian Guitar	6.50	12.50
107	Case to fit	2.25	4.50
KG-21	Arco-Arch Guitar	8.75	17.50
KTG-21	Arco-Arch Tenor Guitar	8.75	17.50
107	Case to fit	2.25	4.50
KG-31	Arco-Arch Guitar	12.50	25.00
KTG-31	Arco-Arch Tenor Guitar	12.50	25.00
119	Case to fit	2.50	5.00

MANDOLINS

KM-11	Mandolin	$ 6.25	$12.50
KM-21	Arco-Arch Mandolin	8.75	17.50
99	Case to fit	1.75	3.50

Nov. 6, 1938

...and prices on Montgomery Ward Instruments – For 1939 Spring ... catalog.

	NET
Recording King Guitar – Carson Robison	$ 5.98
" " " " " Hawaiian	5.98
" " " " " 3/4 size	5.98
" " "	11.50
" " "	12.25
" " "	14.00
" " "	23.00
" " "	30.56
" " " – Ray Whitley model	17.50
" " Tenor Banjo	14.15
" " 5 string Banjo	14.30

...King Electric Hawaiian Guitar outfit ... price – Guitar $ 9.51, Amplifier 17.79 — 27.30

...King Electric Spanish Guitar outfit ... price – #1010 Guitar $13.59, #1009 Amplifier 22.41 — 36.00

...King Roy Smeck model Elec. Spanish outfit ... price – #1127 Guitar $16.88, #1013 Amplifier 24.90 — 41.78

...King Electric Hawaiian Guitar outfit (for #1007 outfit) ... price – #1008 Guitar $12.59, #1020 Amplifier 22.41 — 35.00

...Roy Smeck model Elec. Hawaiian outfit (for #1011 outfit) ... – #1023 (old #1151) Guitar $16.60, #1022 Amplifier 24.90 — 41.50

Neil Abrams

May 3, 1930

KEL KROYDON PRICE LIST AND ORDER BLANK

DATE 5/3/30

SHIP TO

ADDRESS

CITY AND STATE

QUANTITY	STYLE	NET
	KK-1 Guitar	
	KK-2 Guitar	
	Case Extra	
	KK-10 Banjo (Including Case)	
	KK-11 Banjo (Including Case)	
	KK-20 Mandolin	
	KK-21 Mandolin	
	Case Extra	
	KK-1 Guitar	
	KK-2 Guitar	
	Case Extra	
	KK-10 Banjo (Including ...	
	KK-11 Banjo (Including ...	
	KK-20 Mandolin	
	KK-21 Mandolin	
	Case Extra	

MONTGOMERY WARD & CO.

Prices for 1936 Spring and Summer Catalog

Prices effective immediately

These prices cancel all previous prices for these instruments.

Neil Abrams

c1936 Gibson workforce outside the Kalamazoo factory

The Story of Orville Gibson - The Man, The Instrument

Reprint of a 1937 article By Henry J. Dornbush

The story of Gibson instruments and their early creation by Orville H. Gibson, the forming of the present company, the improvements that have been made, and the reputation they have attained is of such an interesting nature that I am going to tell you all about it.

I knew Gibson when I was a boy in my teens. He used to be a clerk in a shoe store here in Kalamazoo, but as a hobby or sideline, he would utilize every opportunity to carve or whittle a piece of wood, finally having a little shop of his own, a room about ten by twelve feet square where he carried out his ideas, the one of most interest to us being that of the making of a mandolin of the violin idea of construction with carved top and back with the Stradivarius arching. His first mandolins were designed along the lines of the present "A" models. The guitars were along the conventional lines of a guitar but with the carved top and back idea like the mandolins. This was back in the 1870's and 1880's.

He made the rim from a thick board, drawing the outside line of the rim on it, and then sawing and carving the inside and outside parts away from the outline of the rim with the result that he had a solid sawed-out rim. The top and back were carved out of solid boards by hand with chisels and gauges and then filed and sandpapered to the desired thickness. Gibson had no power tools and nothing but a hammer, saw, chisel, file, gauge, screw driver and similar tools; probably not even a dream of the wonderful machinery that will roughly carve out a guitar top or back in a few moments. He probably did not even conceive that it would be possible to make mandolins and guitars other than by hand exclusively.

The tops of his mandolins and guitars were carved on the inside and the outside while the backs of the instruments were flat outside, but with a curvature on the inside; the outside having an extension or shape that made it pan-shaped, deep with slanting side walls. The necks were made hollow, tube like, with the idea that this helped create more tonal quality adding more air chamber to the instrument.

The material from which Gibson made his instruments was gathered from wherever he could get it. For instance, the mandolin he made for me, an "F" model back in 1901, was made from some black walnut woodwork in the old Dewing Block. Old furniture was often used by him to make an instrument. He considered this class of wood well seasoned. Walnut, cedar, and spruce were the woods he usually used, the fingerboards being made of cedar.

The first variation Gibson made from the "A" model was the Lyre-shaped mandolin, a picture of which he had on a label that he placed in all the instruments he made. I believe he made only one of these Lyre-shaped instruments and that is owned by J.W. McLouth of Grand Rapids Michigan. His next variation was the style that is now called "F" or Artist's Model.

In graduation the tops and backs he would tap them with his knuckle and carve them more or less until they were in tune with each other. Most of his instruments were made of one-piece tops and backs, but he was not always able to secure the wood he desired, so made quite a number of two-piece top and back instruments. For finishing his instruments he used only varnish; no stains, the natural color of the wood taking care of that. It usually took him from four to six weeks to make a mandolin or guitar and he rarely had more than two or three instruments under construction at one time. I doubt if he made six or eight of the "F" model instruments.

It might be of interest at this point to note that the reputation of his instruments was spreading, and one firm in Boston, requesting the cost, terms, and possible shipping date for 500 mandolins Gibson is his characteristic way replied that it would cost them $100 an instrument and that it would take 500 years for delivery. He never dreamed that the day would come when shipping from 500 to 1000 Gibson instruments a week would be an actual happening. He could not picture quality workmanship and quantity production at the same time as it really exists today.

Orville H. Gibson's original workshop, photographed in 1900 by Mr. Dornbush

The guitars [Orville] Gibson made were large bodied with large sound holes. The thickness of his instruments varied as he kept experimenting for tonal quality and quantity, probably not two instruments being exactly alike in all details. The scale length of his instruments was close to fifteen inches (they are now 13 7/8 inches). The necks were very large and almost clumsy because of the tube-like construction. These long scale lengths caused him quite a lot of grief because of string breakage, which later caused the scale length to be shortened.

The pearl inlays Gibson used were made by a Turkish manufacturer in Grand Rapids, which probably accounts for the star and crescent design used on the instruments he made. It is no wonder that Gibson was interested in the making of guitars and mandolins as he was quite talented on the guitar doing considerable accompaniment work with a well-known local vocal quartet, one of whom was "Ted" McHugh, one of the oldest men in point of service with the Gibson organization today. Gibson's workshop was a regular meeting place or "hangout" for the musicians "about town".

He [Orville] was a bachelor and peculiar in some of his ideas. It is often said that inventors are, or get that way, having visions or dreams of their inventions that others cannot visualize or comprehend. He had great contempt for his competitors often saying that, "they did not know which end of a board to notch in order to make a boot-jack". But, in back of all his peculiarities he had an idea, that unknown to him was to revolutionize the making of mandolins and guitars, and which was to develop into worldwide renown.

During the 1890's, others became interested in his idea with the result that the Gibson Mandolin-Guitar

Company was incorporated in 1902 with Sylvo Reams as General Manager. The firm was later changed to Gibson Inc. On more than one occasion, Sylvo had me bring my Gibson mandolin down to the office to play for someone he wanted to interest in the new instruments. To say that the new idea in construction "took hold" is putting it mildly. Today, the Italian or bowl-shaped mandolin or "the potato bug" is almost a thing of the past. Shortly after forming the company, agencies were established all over the country. Today, the instruments are shipped to and played in every civilized nation of the world.

c1905 Gibson's work force

I recently had the pleasure of going through the present plant of Gibson, Inc. and Wonder of Wonders!!! - From a little 10' x 12' room, one man force, making not over a dozen instruments a year, I saw a building that occupied almost half a city block, with a great lumber yard adjoining, employing over two hundred people and shipping as high as three thousand instruments a month. And the methods used! - From a saw, hammer, chisel and file, I saw great machines that cut large boards into smaller lengths and smooth them. One machine in particular that roughly carved out a guitar top in the matter of only a few moments, after which experts graduate it by hand to the proper thickness; the same handwork that [Orville] Gibson considered so essentially to good tonal quality. I saw a machine that would bend a thick banjo rim in less than a minute, and big forms that would hold the rims and tops and backs in shape while the glue was drying. It was astounding the pain-staking care used on each and every operation throughout the factory. Gibson himself could not have been more particular.

The lumberyard contained woods from all over the world; ebony from Madagascar; rosewood from Brazil, mahogany from Central America, and maple from Michigan and New York, and spruce from The Adirondacks in New York State. The ebony is so precious that it is bought by the pound instead of the usual board foot. After being cut into smaller lengths, these woods went into a great drying room to be further seasoned then the cutting and shaping into instruments started, a thousand and on operations, soon changing the numerous pieces of wood into mandolins, guitars, and banjos.

The finishing of these instruments into beautiful works of art, highly polished and color-blended was also done by experts. In fact, the entire force is a great collection of experts, each in his own particular line. Some of these men have been with the company from 20 - 30 years. No wonder they know how to do their work so well. I saw the testing and final inspection of these instruments before being polished and packed up for shipping. This work is done by men who have had actual, practical experience in orchestra, radio and stage work. They really know what a play needs in an instrument. They place quality ahead of everything. And that is why the instruments have the reputation that is world-known.

It is a literal fact that Gibson gets its materials from all over the world, shapes them into instruments, and then ships the completed instruments all over [the world] - England, Holland, Denmark, Sweden, South Africa,

Australia, New Zealand, South America, India, China, Japan, Philippines, Hawaii, and to all continents. One man's vision or dream of a new principle of construction for mandolins and guitars has made his name "Gibson" famous, a name when spoken of in regard to fretted instruments meaning only one thing, the ultimate of perfection that is Gibson.

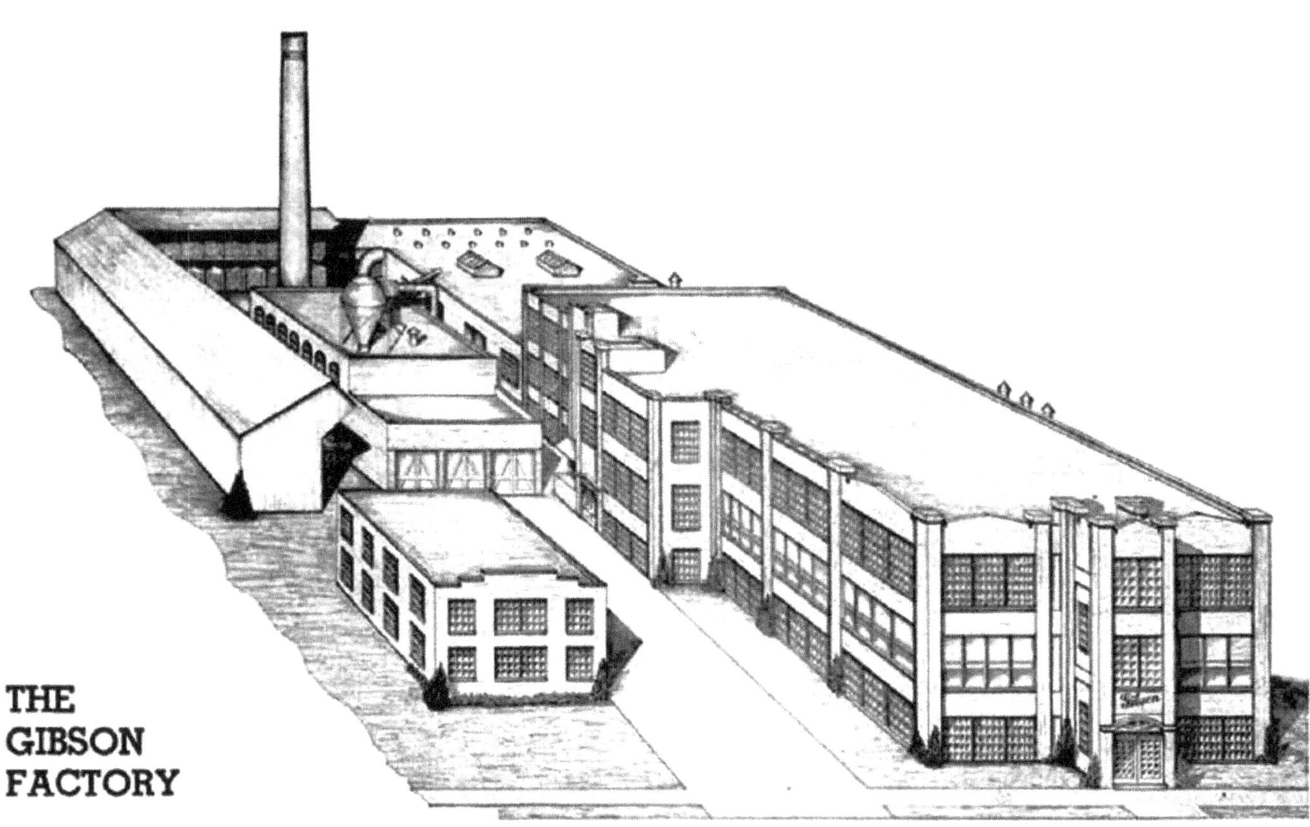

THE GIBSON FACTORY

Ambassador - 1936

Walter Gretsch and William Brenner established the wholesale musical merchandise firm of Gretsch & Brenner in New York City in the 1920's. Walter Gretsch was the brother of Fred Gretsch, manufacturer of Gretsch guitars, and had previously been associated with his brother's company. In 1924, he decided to go out on his own and started Gretsch & Brenner as a manufacturer's agent and importer of European musical merchandise. G&B never manufactured any instruments and was purely a musical instrument wholesale and retail operation. In March 1936, Gibson shipped a quantity of 15 Model M-9 archtop guitars called the "Ambassador" brand. The origin of that brand name is unclear, and the production run was limited to only two separate orders totaling 76 instruments. Gibson shipping ledgers indicate that they were four different model guitars and two mysterious other models C-5 and C-7, which are unknown in terms of design or type of instrument. There are surviving examples of the M-9 even though there were only a total of 27 ordered.

Models:

M-5 Archtop guitar
(similar to Cromwell G-4)

M-7 Archtop guitar
(similar to Cromwell G-5)

M-9 Archtop guitar (peg head design shown below)
(similar to Cromwell G-6)

M-11 Archtop guitar
(similar to Cromwell G-8)

C-5 unknown model
C-7 unknown model

A March 1936 Gibson shipping ledger entry for the Ambassador models

18-M-5 482-B-1- 482-B-24
482-B-11-482-B-44
482-B-42-482-B-9 482-B-27
482-B-40-482-B-39-482-B-25
482-B-36-482-B-5-482-B-56
482-B-18-482-B-3-482-B-12
482-B-34-482-B-14
6-M-7 483-B-16 483-B-20
483-B-10-483-B-19
483-B-11-483-B-22
484-B-7-484-B-1
12-M-9- 484-B-9-484-B-4
484-B-15-484-B-23-484-B-30
484-B-21-484-B-18-484-B-26
484-B-28-484-B-10
485-B-1-485-B-5-485-B-12
5-M-11- 485-B-5-485-B-8
10-C-7
10-C-5
Gretsch & Brenner

Capital - 1937-1938

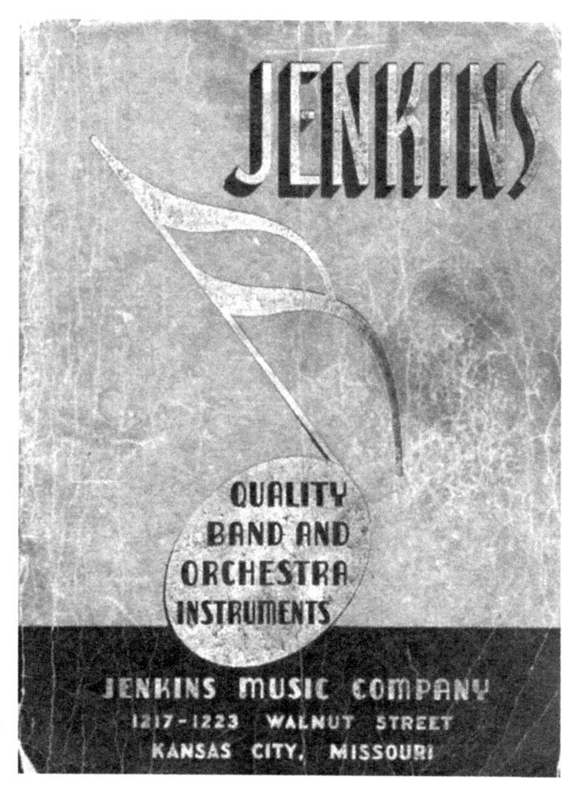

The Jenkins Music Co., Kansas City, MO., was one of the largest wholesalers and retailers of musical goods in the entire country. Jenkins Co. operated stores in St. Joseph and Joplin Missouri; Topeka, Wichita, Leavenworth, Independence, and Salina, Kansas; Tulsa, Seminole, Oklahoma City, and Bartlesville, Oklahoma; Fort Smith, Arkansas and Amarillo, Texas. At the height of the Great Depression the company employed more than 500 people at its various locations. They were also one of Gibson's largest distributors carrying the full Gibson and Kalamazoo line. Beginning in 1936, JW Jenkins had Gibson produce their own in-house brand called "Capital". They were essentially re-labeled Cromwell models with the Capital brand name stenciled on the headstock.

The model numbers of the majority of Capitals started with "J" for Jenkins, but the model numbers changed in mid-1937, making it a bit more difficult to decipher the Gibson shipping ledger entries. For example, the Model J-1, which was a re-labeled Cromwell G-2 flattop guitar, changed to Model J-15 in July 1937. The best selling model was the J-2 or J-16, which was the same as the Cromwell G-4 archtop guitar totaling 140 units.

THE NEW JENKINS BUILDING

The J-1 and J-15s totaled 75 guitars. Gibson also made electric instruments for Jenkins including archtop guitars, lap steels, and mandolins some of which correspond to similar Cromwell models, but others like the EJ-3 do not. Some of these odd model numbers can be attributed to errors in Gibson's own shipping records and may not be different models at all. Since there a few surviving examples and no known copies of J.W. Jenkins catalogs from this era, also use the chapter on Cromwell as a reference for the different models listed on the following page.

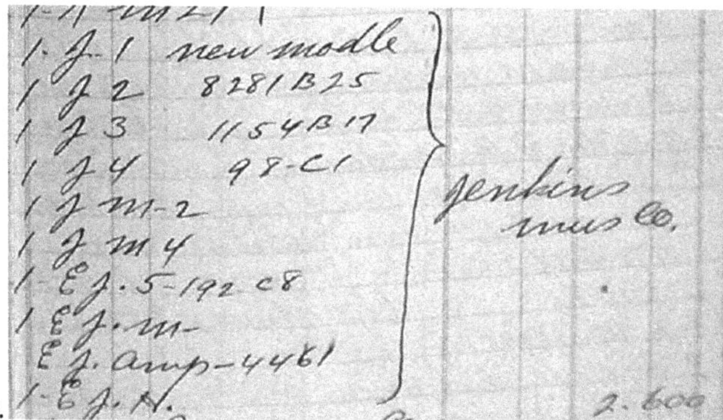

Right: 1937 Gibson shipping ledger entry for Capital-brand instruments.

Capital Models:

J-1 & J-15 Flattop guitars
(Similar to the Cromwell G-2)

J-2 & J-16 - Archtop guitars
(Similar to the Cromwell G-4)

J-3 & J-17 - Archtop guitars
(Similar to the Cromwell G-5)

J-4 & J-18 & J-19 - Archtop Guitars
(Similar to the Cromwell G-6)

JTG, JTG-2 Tenor guitars
(Similar to the Cromwell GT-4 tenor)

EJ-3 & EJ-5 - Electric Spanish Guitar
(Similar to the Cromwell EG-5)

EJ-H - Electric Hawaiian Lap steel guitar
(Similar to the Cromwell EG-H)

JM-2 - Mandolin
(Similar to the Cromwell GM-2)

JM-4 - Mandolin
(Similar to the Cromwell GM-4)

EJM - Electric Mandolin
(Similar to the Cromwell EGM)

Captial Model J-1

Captial Model J-2

Captial Model J-3

Coast Wholesale - Henry L. Mason - 1936-1939

Coast Wholesale was a west coast musical instrument distributor based in San Francisco and Los Angeles who had taken over Sherman Clay & Co. in the 1920's. Gibson made the Henry L. Mason branded guitars, which were the same as the Cromwell acoustic guitars of the same time period. The only difference is the stenciled logo on the peghead. This allowed Gibson to build all of these brands at the same time and only change the stenciled logo and add the 'CW' prefix to the model number. Since there are few surviving examples and no known copies of Coast Wholesale's catalogs from this era, use the chapter on Cromwell as a reference for the different models listed below.

Below: The headstock of the Henry L. Mason brand Model CWTG-4

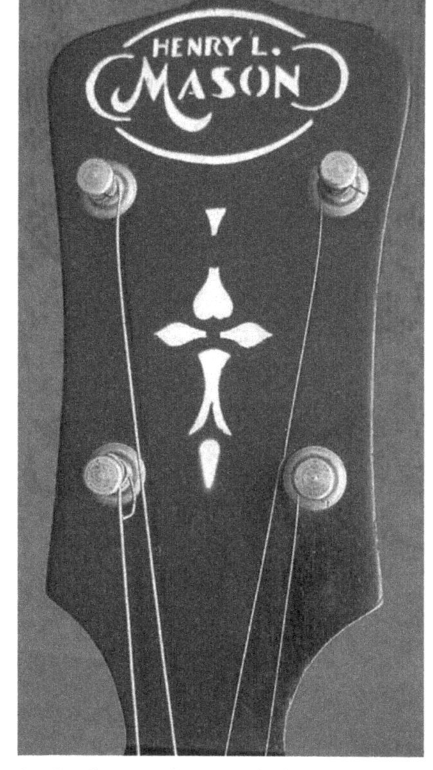

Mason CW-2 Flattop guitar
(Similar to the Cromwell G-2)

Mason CW-4 Arch-top guitar
(Similar to the Cromwell G-4)

Mason CW-5 Arch-top guitar
(Similar to the Cromwell G-5)

Mason CW-6 Arch-top guitar
(Similar to the Cromwell G-6)

Mason CWT-2 or CWTG-2 flattop tenor guitar
(Similar to the Cromwell GT-4)

Mason CWT-4 or CWTG-4 flattop tenor guitar
(Similar to the Cromwell GT-4)

Mason CWM-2 mandolin
(Similar to the Cromwell GM-2)

Mason CWM-4 mandolin
(Similar to the Cromwell GM-4)

Mason CWM-5 mandolin
Unknown model

Mason CWM-6 mandolin
Unknown model

Below: An April 1936 shipping ledger entry for Coast Wholesale

24 C.W-4 434-13-434-17-434-10
434-5-434-16-434-23
434-18-434-21-434-20
434-22-434-6-434-43
434-46-434-18-363-a-14
434-41-434-24-373-a-58
363-a-100-434-42-434-373-a-93
373-a-15-373-a-40-363-23
116 Coast Wholesale (Los angeles)
4/2/36

Chapter 5

Cromwell - 1935-1939

In 1935, Gibson started manufacturing another in-house budget brand called Cromwell. Unlike the Kalamazoo brand, Gibson hid the fact that they were "Gibson" made, opting for phrases like "Guitars By Master Craftsmen". Gibson wanted to maintain the "Gibson" name as the best brand (and most expensive), while offering the Cromwell line as a separate brand name for less cost; kind of like Michelin making all Sears-brand tires. Other than Kalamazoo, Cromwell was basically Gibson's other primary house brand. Mainly, the idea was to have a line of guitars that Gibson could sell to jobbers (large musical instrument distributor that carried many brands), who in turn would re-sell to music stores who weren't franchised Gibson dealers and couldn't get the full Gibson line, but had a market for less expensive versions like the Cromwells.

Continental Music (owned by C.G. Conn) sold the highest number of Cromwells totaling 829 instruments for the years 1936 to 1940. Others included Grossman's Music in Cleveland, OH, J.W Jenkins in Kansas City, Coast Wholesale in Los Angeles, Gretsch & Brenner (not to be confused with Gretsch Guitars), New York Band Instrument. The largest distributors of the Cromwell line were Continental Music and Grossman's Music.

The G-2 flattop is quite rare and few exist making them more valuable. The arch-tops G-4 and G-6 were the most popular, and many examples still exist, but are not as valuable. In 1936, the Model G-8 was introduced as the top of the line, but the higher price hurt sales, and was discontinued soon after, which makes it one of the most valuable and collectable Cromwells. The difference between the models was based on the Model number (low to high). The G-4 was the least expensive; the G-6 had an inlaid logo and fancier black & white checkered purfling (similar to the Kalamazoo KG-32). All had Gibson tailpieces, but usually Grover-made pickguard brackets and the most recognizable feature all the Cromwells, besides the large stenciled logo on the peghead, was a white stripe running down the center of the fingerboard. Most experts agree that Gibson probably made the Cromwell brand starting in early 1935, but stopped sometime in late 1938, or possibly early 1939.

Cromwell Distributors

Continental Music - Chicago, IL
In 1939-1930, the C. G. Conn band instrument company greatly expanded its product lines, including their acquisition of Ludwig percussion, Carl Fischer's musical instrument department, and the Soprani Company, makers of accordions. The also owned the Elkhart Band Instrument Company, Leedy percussion, and 49.9% of H. & A. Selmer's stock, acquired during the consolidation of Conn's New York joint venture with Selmer. Conn also acquired a wholesale distribution company in 1930, Continental Music Company, which was begun in 1923 as a wholesale division of Conn's Chicago retail store and the Pan American Band Instrument Company. This made Continental one of the largest mid-west musical instrument distributor, as well as the largest distributor for the Cromwell brand selling more than 800 units from 1935 to 1940.

Grossman's Music - Cleveland, OH
Henry Grossman, a local Cleveland, Ohio music retailer wanted to expand his operations into wholesale musical instrument sales as well, founded Grossman's Music in 1922. They issued very large catalogs that contained many different brands of instruments including the Gibson and Cromwell lines. They sold nearly 500 Cromwells from 1935-1938.

Gretsch & Brenner - New York, NY - (also see Chapter 2 on Ambassador)
G&B was not a large distributor of Cromwells selling only 112 units from 1936 to 1937.

New York Band Instrument - New York, NY
New York Band Instrument Co. was an off-shoot of Gretsch & Brenner as the small goods retail store in New York City. They were also a distributor of the main Gibson line, as well as Kalamazoos. From 1935-1940, NY Band sold well over 400 Cromwell guitars and mandolins.

Davitt & Hanser - Cincinnati, OH
William Davitt and John F. Hanser Sr., both of whom had previously worked at a Wurlitzer music store in Cincinnati, launched Davitt & Hanser in 1924 as a wholesale/retail operation. After Davitt's untimely death John Hanser took over the running of the company. Hanser Sr. was then succeeded by his two sons John Jr. and Robert and a son-in-law, Elmer Dansberry. Davitt & Hanser Distributing began as a family-run business serving the retail music stores in the local area. Today, the third generation family-run Hanser Music Group serves over 5,000 customers around the world and manages such brands as B.C. Rich. Back in the 1930's, they sold well over 300 Cromwells from 1935-1938.

Beare & Sons - London, England
Originally established in England in 1865, R.B. Beare was a family company of violin restorers and dealers and the oldest musical instrument dealer in the UK. In 1892, the business was split into Beare & Sons, musical retailer, and Beare, Goodwin & Co. Beare & Sons was originally managed by founder John Beare's younger son, Walter. In 1931, Walter's son, John Barrington Beare took over as managing director and concentrated on selling a larger assortment of new musical instruments including Gibson and Cromwell guitars. They sold over 200 Cromwells from 1935-1937.

L.D. Heater - Seattle, WA
L.D. Heater was a music retailer & wholesaler with locations in Seattle, WA and Portland, OR. They distributed the Cromwell brand, but also had Gibson re-label many as their own in-house brand "Hayden". The Hayden brand model number did not differ from the Cromwell models making it very difficult to differentiate between the two. They sold over 200 Cromwells from 1935-1938.

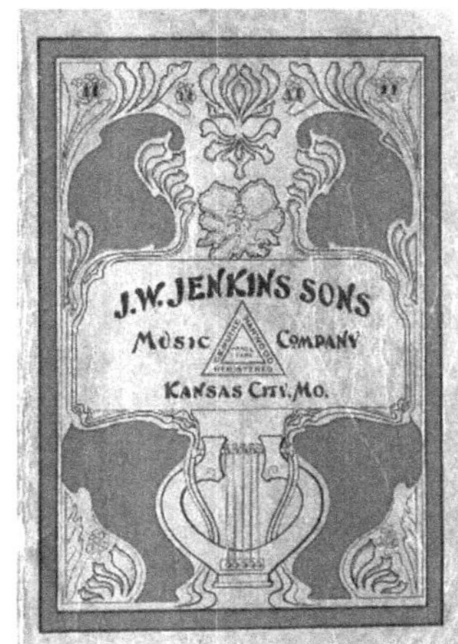

J.W. Jenkins - Kansas City, MO (also see Chapter 3 on Capital)
The Jenkins music Co., Kansas City, MO., sold some of the Cromwell-branded instruments in 1936, prior to having Gibson make their own in-house brand, "Capital". There were also one of the largest wholesalers and retailers of Gibsons in the entire mid-west. They sold only 27 Cromwells in 1936.

Francis, Day & Hunter - (also see Chapter 6 on FDH)
FD&H was Gibson's largest distributor in the England for the entire Gibson line, Kalamazoo and Cromwell, as well as their own custom brand "The FDH Special". They sold approximately 457 Cromwells from 1936-1939.

Cromwell Models and Specifications:

G-2 Flat-top Guitar - 1935-1940
Body 14 ¾" x 19 ¼" (similar to the Kalamazoo KG-14)
Mahogany back, sides and neck, "white" spruce top
14-fret neck, Rosewood FB with white center stripe.
RW pin bridge with white pins
"Cream" single bound top, back & sound hole
Glued on tortoise shell pickguard
Slanted "roof peak" peg head with stenciled logo
Brown mahogany B&S & sunburst top

G-4 Arch-top Guitar - 1935-1939
Body: 16" x 20 ¼" (similar to Gibson L-50)
Mahogany back, sides and neck, spruce top
Arco-arch back & top
14-fret neck, spruce top
Single bound top & back only
Rosewood FB with white center stripe. RW adjustable bridge
Elevated tortoise shell pickguard
Slanted "roof peak" peg head shape with stenciled Cromwell logo
Two-tone mahogany B&S, sunburst top

G-5 Arch-top Guitar - 1935-1939 (not pictured)
Same body as G-4
Mahogany back, sides and 14-fret neck
Carved X-braced spruce top
Single bound top & back
Rosewood FB with white center stripe
RW adjustable bridge
Elevated tortoise shell pickguard
Slanted "roof peak" peg head with stenciled logo
Dark brown B&S & sunburst top

Cromwell G-5

G-6 Arch-top Guitar - 1935-1939
Same body as G-5
Mahogany back, sides and 14-fret neck
Arco-arch back & top
Top & back bound with B&W checkered celluloid
Rosewood FB with white center stripe
RW adjustable bridge
Bound Elevated tortoise shell pickguard
Slanted "roof peak" peg head with Cromwell logo
Dark brown B&S & sunburst top

Cromwell GT-4

Cromwell G-8

G-8 Arch-top Guitar - 1935-1936
Same body as G-6
Mahogany back, sides and 14-fret neck, spruce top
Top & back bound with B&W checkered celluloid
Rosewood FB with white center stripe &
small diamond pattern inlays
RW adjustable bridge
Slanted "roof peak" peg head shape with
inlaid Cromwell logo & large "arrowhead"
Bound Elevated tortoise shell pickguard
Dark brown B&S & sunburst top

GT-4 Tenor Guitar 1935-1939
Same body as G-4
4-string tenor guitar neck

EG-5 Electric Guitar - 1937-1938
An electric version of the G-5 arch-top guitar
Oval pickup with bar in middle position
Bound Elevated tortoise shell pickguard with cut-out for pickup
(Also available with 4-string tenor neck as Model EGT-5)

EG-H Electric Hawaiian Guitar - 1937-1938
Small lap steel electric (similar to Gibson EH-150)
Pear-shaped body with narrow shoulders
Curly Maple top & back
Blade-style pickup with oval cover plate

EG-Amp
(similar to c1938 Gibson EH-100)
10" speaker & 6 tubes

GM-2 Mandolin - 1935-1939
Flat-backed mandolin with round hole
Single bound top & back
Rosewood FB with white center stripe & dot markers
Tortoise shell pickguard
RW adjustable bridge
Slanted "roof peak" peg head with stenciled logo
Dark brown B&S & golden sunburst top

GM-4 Mandolin - 1935-1939
Gibson A style body with f-holes
Single bound top & back
Rosewood FB with white center stripe & dot markers
Elevated tortoise shell pickguard
RW adjustable bridge
Slanted "roof peak" peg head with stenciled logo
Dark brown B&S & golden sunburst top

No. GM-2

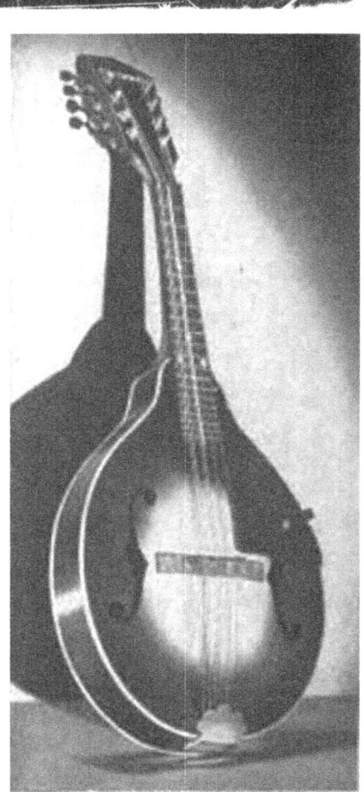

GM-4

Francis, Day & Hunter - 1937-1940

Musical instrument distributor Francis, Day & Hunter was founded in 1877 by William & James Francis, David Day, and Harry Hunter. Their music store was located on a well-known thoroughfare, Charing Cross Road in West Central London. In the 1930's, they were the largest UK distributor for Gibson selling the entire Gibson line of flattop, archtop, and electric guitars, banjos, mandolins and ukuleles, as well as the Cromwell brand. In May 1937 FD&H ordered 18 custom-made Gibsons that would be branded as the "NEW Style FDH", also referred to as the "FDH Special". It was very similar to the Montgomery Ward Recording King M-5, and touted as "The Guitar That Gives You Everything, specially constructed to meet the requirements of British Guitarists". No other Gibson-made guitar could ever make that claim. Its appointments included the very M-5-like "pointed dome" peghead shape; "bull's eye" shaped fingerboard and headstock inlays; checker- board binding. In all, Gibson shipped 123 FDH Specials from 1937 to 1940 and all but eight were shipped directly to Francis, Day & Hunter. The last six were sold to Davitt & Hanser, a US-based Gibson distributor, presumably leftover stock no longer wanted by FD&H.

This rare 1937-38 page came from a UK Gibson catalog and contains the only known illustration and description of the Style FDH.

NEW!

STYLE FDH

Carved Top

FEATURES

Wood: Body of finest curly maple; genuine carved top graduated to a thousandth part of an inch to give the finest quality of tone and power; new black and white checker binding: mahogany neck with rosewood fingerboard

Finish and Decorations: Highly finished to bring out the beautiful grain in the wood. Bound fingerboard, large fancy inlays.

Fittings: Genuine ebony adjustable bridge; nickel plated individual machine heads; improved nickel extension tailpiece; elevated finger-rest.

Body Size: Grand Auditorium—16¼ inches wide and 20¼ inches long.

★ Price £18 : 18 : 0

Including Case

Hire Purchase Terms:
Deposit £1 1s. 0d. and 18 monthly instalments of £1 3s. 6d
or Deposit £1 1s. 0d. and 78 weekly instalments of 5s. 8d.

THE GUITAR THAT GIVES YOU EVERYTHING!

Specially constructed to meet the requirements of British Guitarists, the new Gibson FDH Special model is a revelation.

In this new model GIBSON have achieved the seemingly impossible—maximum volume and cutting power but combined with the distinctive and world famous GIBSON depth and beauty of tone.

Suitable alike for orchestral or solo work.

Guitar Model:

Style FDH Arch-top guitar - 1936-1937
Body 16 ¼" x 20 ¼" (same as Recording King M-5)
Curly maple veneer back & sides - carved spruce top
Mahogany 14-fret neck with RW fingerboard
"Bulls eye" MOP FB & peghead inlays
Black & white "checkered" top binding
Single bound back, FB & elevated celluloid pickguard
Ebony adjustable bridge (was probably RW)
Nickel tuners & trapeze tailpiece
"Pointed dome" shaped peghead with MOP FDH logo
Mahogany finish with sunburst top

Below: Gibson shipping ledger entry for 10 FDH Specials

1-K EH. Inst DKE. 3607 — Francis Day & Hunter
10- FDH. spl- 8128 9 - 8128 21
8128 22 - 8128 4
8128 6 - 812 810
8128 5 - 8128 7
8128 13 - 8128 14

Chapter 6

Kalamazoo 1933-1942

Trying to battle the effects of the Great Depression and to keep their employees working, Gibson followed the Kel Kroydon toy line with the Kalamazoo branded instruments. They also followed the Kel Kroydon toy line with another subsidiary, The Kalamazoo Playthings Toy Company. Kalamazoo Playthings toys offered many more designs all made of wood that Gibson hoped would also keep manufacturing at near full capacity. Both the Kel Kroydon and Kalamazoo Playthings toy divisions were short-lived, which might indicate that they served their purpose and carried Gibson through some very lean years during 1931-1933. Pictured below, a variation of the "Kala-Kar Milk Wagon" and one of the only known example of a Kalamazoo Playthings toy ever found.

DOUBLE SALES VALUE

NEW PUZZLE BLOCKS IN BRILLIANT, STURDY WAGONS— TRUCKS—and EXPRESS TRAINS

NEW TOYS—NEW PEP IN YOUR SALES

NEW—KALAMAZOO PLAYTHINGS

PUZZLE BLOCKS

WAGONS AND TRUCKS

ALL ABOARD! THE "KPC EXPRE

Here is a brand new puzzle block creation that will make them buy.

KALAMAZOO PLAYTHINGS COMPANY

KALAMAZOO · MICHIGAN

NEW COMPLETE CATALOG

BAKER & BENNETT COMPANY, 200 Fifth Avenue, Room 420, New York

G. E. DALTON COMPANY, 747 Warehouse Street, Los Angeles

Left: c1932 Kalamazoo Playthings sales flyer

The Kalamazoo brand of instruments would turn out to be the most successful of Gibson's in-house budget brands, manufacturing guitars, banjos, mandolins, mandolas, mando-cellos, mando-basses, and the entire violin family of instruments from 1933 - 1942. Gibson did resurrect the Kalamazoo brand after WWII for a brief time in the 1950's and then again in the late 1960's, but the vast majority was manufactured during the pre-war era. The Kalamazoo brand was marketed as one flyer states as "The World's Greatest Value" and introduced the Model KG (Kalamazoo Guitar) renamed the KG-11 in 1934; the KTG-11 a 4-string tenor guitar; the KM or KM-11 (Kalamazoo mandolin); the KTB (Kalamazoo Tenor Banjo); KPB (Plectrum Banjo) and KRB (Kalamazoo Regular Banjo) Gibson always referred to their 5-string banjos as "regular".

In 1934, they also introduced the KM-21 a fancier version of the KM-11 mandolin with f-holes and an elevated pickguard, and an arch-top guitar model KG-31. The Kalamazoo arch-tops featured Gibson's "Arco-arch" back, which was a fancy term for pressed or molded plywood with a mahogany or maple veneer. In 1936, Gibson made a "Hawaiian" version of the KG-11 - the KHG-11 (Kalamazoo Hawaiian Guitar), as well as the KG-21 a smaller arch-top similar to the Gibson L-30. Probably the most well known model was the KG-14, which was almost exactly like Gibson's legendary 1930's flattop models L-1, L-0, and L-00 (minus a truss rod and different interior bracing) and also made a Hawaiian version (KHG-14) and a tenor guitar (KTG-14). The flattops were all made out of solid wood up to about 1938-39, which makes them more valuable in today's market compared to the arch-top guitars. In 1937, Gibson introduced the KG-3/4 as a "new guitar for children" and then re-named the Kalamazoo Sport, which could be considered one of the first-ever travel guitars.

Gibson also produced a full-line of instruments in the mandolin family including the Kalamazoo KH-21 & KH-22 mandolas, KK-31 mando-cello, and the KJ mando-bass, and even a violin model mirroring their Gibson cousins.

c1933 Kalamazoo sales flyer

The most expensive and ornate Kalamazoo guitars was the KG-32, introduced in 1939 as less expensive alternative to Gibson's L-50. The KG-32 had a 16" wide solid spruce arched top with a "flashy" black & white checkered purfling, and later the KGN-32 "Oriole", an all natural finish version in 1940. Also in 1940, the KGN-12 (similar to the KG-14) also nicknamed "Oriole", because of the Oriole bird decal on the peghead, below the Kalamazoo script logo. The "Oriole" models were only made in 1940-42, and had "flamed maple" back sides and faux tortoise-shell bindings.

When Gibson introduced the world to its new "electric guitar" models in 1936, they followed suit in 1939 with Kalamazoo models KEH (Kalamazoo Electric Hawaiian) and KEH-R (KEH packaged with an amplifier); the KES (Kalamazoo Electric Spanish), which looked like the KGN-12 with a sound hole pickup installed. The later version of the KES (c1940) closely resembled the c1937 Gibson ES-100 with an arched-top body and f-holes, and the pickup mounted in the bridge position.

The Kalamazoo brand was sold strictly "wholesale" generally with a minimum of two of the same model at a time, but was mostly ordered in larger quantities. They were distributed either through existing Gibson dealers or smaller music stores that didn't carry the more expensive guitars. Gibson also sold a line of Kalamazoo strings, but in 1942 after the start of WWII, Gibson discontinued the Kalamazoo brand until a brief period in the 1950's and 1960's when the name was re-introduced for a brief time on a small line of electric guitars, basses, and amplifiers.

Kalamazoo Models:

KG or KG-11 Flattop Guitar - 1933-1938
Body: 14 ¾" x 17 ½"
Mahogany B&S, Spruce Top
RW fingerboard & bridge
Flat peghead shape with Kalamazoo logo
14-fret neck

KG-11

KTG-11 Flattop tenor guitar - 1933-1938 (not shown)
Same body as KG-11
Short 23" scale length
Friction tuning pegs (same as banjos)
Flat peghead shape with Kalamazoo silk-screened logo

KHG-11 Flattop Hawaiian guitar - 1933-1938
Same body as KG-11
12-fret wide neck
Elevated strings
Flat peghead shape with Kalamazoo silk-screened logo

KHG-11

KG-16 Arch-top guitar - 1937-1942
Same body as KG-21 - 14 ½" W x 19 ¼" L
Mahogany arch-arch back & solid sides
Arco-arched spruce top
Finished in NEW "mist-brown"
Ivoroid bound top & back
Elevated celluloid pickguard
14-fret mahogany neck with "steel rod"
Domed peg head shape with pointy top

KG-12 Flattop guitar - 1937-1942
Same body size as KG-14 - 14 ¾" x 19 ¼"
Natural mahogany B&S, spruce top
(brown-mist sunburst)
Rosewood FB & bridge with black pins
14-fret neck
3-on-plate style tuners with black buttons
Glued on celluloid pickguard
Domed peg head shape with pointy top

KHG-12 - 1939 (not shown)
(Same as KG-12 but with 12-fret Hawaiian neck)

KGN-12 "Oriole" - 1940-1941
(Same body as KG-14)
Flamed solid maple sides
Maple veneer back, spruce top
Natural finish with faux tortoise-shell binding
Most had Gibson-style "open book" peg head shape
Kalamazoo logo with Oriole bird decal

KHG-12 - 1939 (not shown)
(Same as KG-12 but with 12-fret Hawaiian neck)

KG-14 Flattop guitar - 1936-1939
Body: 14 ¾" x 19 1/2" (similar to Gibson L-00)
Brown mahogany B&S, sunburst spruce top
Rosewood FB & bridge with black pins
14-fret neck & 3-on-plate style tuners with white buttons
Glued on celluloid pickguard
Slanted "roof peak" peg head shape
(Available with tenor neck as Model KTG-14)

KHG-14 Flattop Hawaiian guitar - 1936-1939
Same body as KG-14 - 12-fret wide neck
Slanted "roof peak" peg head shape

Kalamazoo Sport (KG-3/4 size) - 1937-1942
Small body 12 ¾"W x 17 ¼" long
Brown mahogany B&S, sunburst spruce top
Short 15 ½" rosewood FB with 19 frets
RW bridge with black pins
Smaller narrower 14-fret neck
3-on-plate style tuners with black buttons
Ivoroid binding on top only
Glued on celluloid pickguard
Slanted "roof peak" peg head shape

Kalamazoo 'Senior' - 1936-1937 (not shown)
Same as KG-11 - NEVER appeared in any Kalamazoo brochure
Kalamazoo logo with 'Senior" stenciled vertically on the PH
24 1/2" scale length
Firestripe Pickguard

KG-21 Arch-top guitar - 1935-1936
Body 14 ¾" x 19 ¼" with f-holes
(similar to Gibson L-30)
Brown mahogany B&S, sunburst spruce top
Rosewood FB & adjustable bridge
Elevated celluloid pickguard
Pointed "roof peak" peg head shape
(Available with tenor neck as Model KTG-21)

KG-31 Arch-top guitar - 1935-1939
Body 16" x 20 ¼" with f-holes (similar to Gibson L-50)
Brown mahogany B&S, sunburst spruce top
Rosewood FB & adjustable bridge
Elevated celluloid pickguard
Pointed "roof peak" peg head shape
14-fret neck - 24 ¾" scale length
(Available with tenor neck as Model KTG-31)

KG-32 Arch-top guitar - 1937-1942
Same body as KG-31
Curly maple (arch-arch) back & solid sides
Arco-arched spruce top & back
Black & white checkered binding on top
Ivoroid bound back, bound FB & pickguard
14-fret mahogany neck with "steel rod"
Domed peg head shape with pointy top

KG-22 Arch-top guitar - 1937-1942
Same body as KG-31 16" x 20 ¼"
Maple (Arco) back & solid sides
Arco-arched spruce top (sunburst)
Ivoroid bound top & back
Elevated celluloid pickguard
14-fret mahogany neck with "steel rod"
Domed peg head shape with pointy top

KGN-32 "Oriole" (1940-41)
(Same body as KG-32)
Flamed maple sides & veneer back, spruce top
Natural finish with faux tortoise-shell binding
Most had Gibson-style "open book" peg head shape
Kalamazoo and orange Oriole bird silk-screened logos
Domed peg head shape with pointy top

KV-44 Violin - 1939-1942
Carved spruce top
Curly maple back, sides and neck
Ebony fingerboard
Ebony friction tuning pegs

Kalamazoo

KES - Kalamazoo Electric Spanish Flattop Guitar - 1937-1940
Same body as KG-12 & KG-14
Sound hole pickup and single volume control
mounted in the top below the pickguard
¼" phono jack mounted on the side, lower bout

KES - Kalamazoo Electric Spanish Archtop Guitar - 1941-1942
Same body as KG-21 arched-top 14 ¾" x 19 ¼"
Top mounted pickup in the bridge position
Single volume control
¼" phono jack mounted on the side, lower bout

KEH - Kalamazoo Electric Hawaiian - 1937-1939
Lap steel electric (similar to Gibson EH-100)
Single bar pickup with "boomerang" coverplate
1-volume & 1-tone control
Single bound top & back

KEH-R - Kalamazoo Electric Hawaiian - 1937-1942
"Oriole" bird decal on headstock
Un-bound body
Dark brown or "ripple-spun" finish
Packaged with KEA-R amp with
detachable chassis

MODEL KEH
Electric Hawaiian Guitar
Complete $75.00

Instrument	$27.50
Case	$ 5.00
Amplifier	$42.50

KEA and KEH amp
Similar to Gibson EH-100 amp
10" speaker
6 tubes

KEH-R $97.50

Complete Outfit

New AMPLIFIER

Just think! Those troublesome rattles and noises gone forever in a new idea brought to you for the first time by Kalamazoo.

Made in two pieces; the speaker is detachable from the chassis so that when in use, the upper part containing the speaker is detached and set aside; no vibrating of tubes, no rattles.

Only Kalamazoo brings to you such an outfit at so low a price. Big 10" high fidelity speaker. 10 foot detachable cord. 29 frets 4½ octaves.

The pick-up unit has also been improved to make the tone more brilliant and sustain longer in the upper positions.

KEH - Kalamazoo Electric Hawaiian - 1940-1942
"Oriole" bird decal on heastock
"Mist brown" sunburst finish or
"Ripple-spun" amber finish
1-volume & 1-tone control
Un-bound top & back

KEH .. *Electric Hawaiian Guitar*

$85.00

Complete Outfit

NEW AMPLIFIER: Just think! Those troublesome rattles and noises gone forever in a new idea brought to you for the first time by Kalamazoo. Made in two pieces—the speaker is detachable from the chassis so that when in use, the upper part containing the speaker is detached and set aside; no vibrating of tubes, no rattles; big 10" high fidelity speaker; six tubes; plenty of power so as to give satisfactory results as a P. A. System.

NEW, IMPROVED INSTRUMENT: In a brilliantly attractive sunburst finish with new type pickup unit for more power and sustaining quality of tone; matched designs on fingerboard for easier playing of harmonics and octaves; 29 frets give you over 4½ octave range.

KEH Instrument	$30.00
33 Case	5.00
KEA Amplifier	50.00
	$85.00
Amplifier Slip-on Cover, extra	$ 1.75

KH-21 Mandola (1936) and KH-22 Mandola - 1937
A-style body, but slightly larger than a mandolin
Arco-arched top (sunburst), mahogany back & sides
Rosewood FB with Ivoroid binding
Ivoroid binding top & back
Ivoroid bound elevated celluloid pickguard
Pointed "roof peak" peg head shape

KK-31 Mando-cello - 1936
8-string version of the KG-31 guitar
Body 16" x 20 ¼" with f-holes
Arco-arched veneer top - sunburst finish
Mahogany sides, and veneer back
Rosewood FB & adjustable bridge
Elevated celluloid pickguard
Slanted "roof peak" peg head shape
Tuning: A D G C (strings in pairs)

KH-21

KK-31

KK-32 Mando-cello (1937)
Same as KK-31
Curly maple (arch-arch) back & solid sides
Arco-arched spruce top (sunburst)
Ivoroid bound top & back, bound FB & pickguard

KJ Mando-Bass
(Similar to Gibson J mando-bass)
24" wide body x 33 ½" long x 5 ½" deep
Arco-arch top with f-holes
Maple back & sides
Mahogany neck

KM-21 Mandolin - 1933-1936
(A-style body with f-holes)
Rosewood FB with Ivoroid binding
Ivoroid binding top & back
Ivoroid bound elevated celluloid pickguard
Pointed "roof peak" peg head shape

KM-22 Mandolin - 1937-1942
Same as KM-21 except Arco-arched spruce top (sunburst)
Curly maple (Arco) back & solid sides
Pointed "roof peak" peg head shape

KM-11 Mandolin (1933 -
Flat-back Style A mandolin
Round sound hole
Glued on pickguard

KALAMAZOO MANDOLINS

KM-12 Mandolin
Same as KM-11 except
Brown-mist sunburst top
Domed peg head shape with pointy top

KMN-12 "Oriole" Mandolin - 1940-1942
(same body as KM-12)
Natural maple finish
Tortoise shell binding
"Oriole" bird decal on PH

KTB - Kalamazoo Tenor Banjo - 1933-1942
4-string maple neck - 23" scale length - 19 frets
Friction tuning pegs
11" maple rim & 14" resonator
Rogers calfskin head & nickel hardware

KPB - Kalamazoo Plectrum Banjo - 1933-1942 (not shown)
Same rim & resonator as KTB
4-string long neck - 27" scale length - 22 frets

KRB - Kalamazoo Regular Banjo - 1933-1942 (not shown)
Same rim & resonator as KTB
5-string neck (same size as KPB)

KMB - Kalamazoo Mandolin Banjo - 1933-1936 (not shown)
Regular mandolin fingerboard & neck - KTB tenor banjo rim

Kel Kroydon - 1930-1932

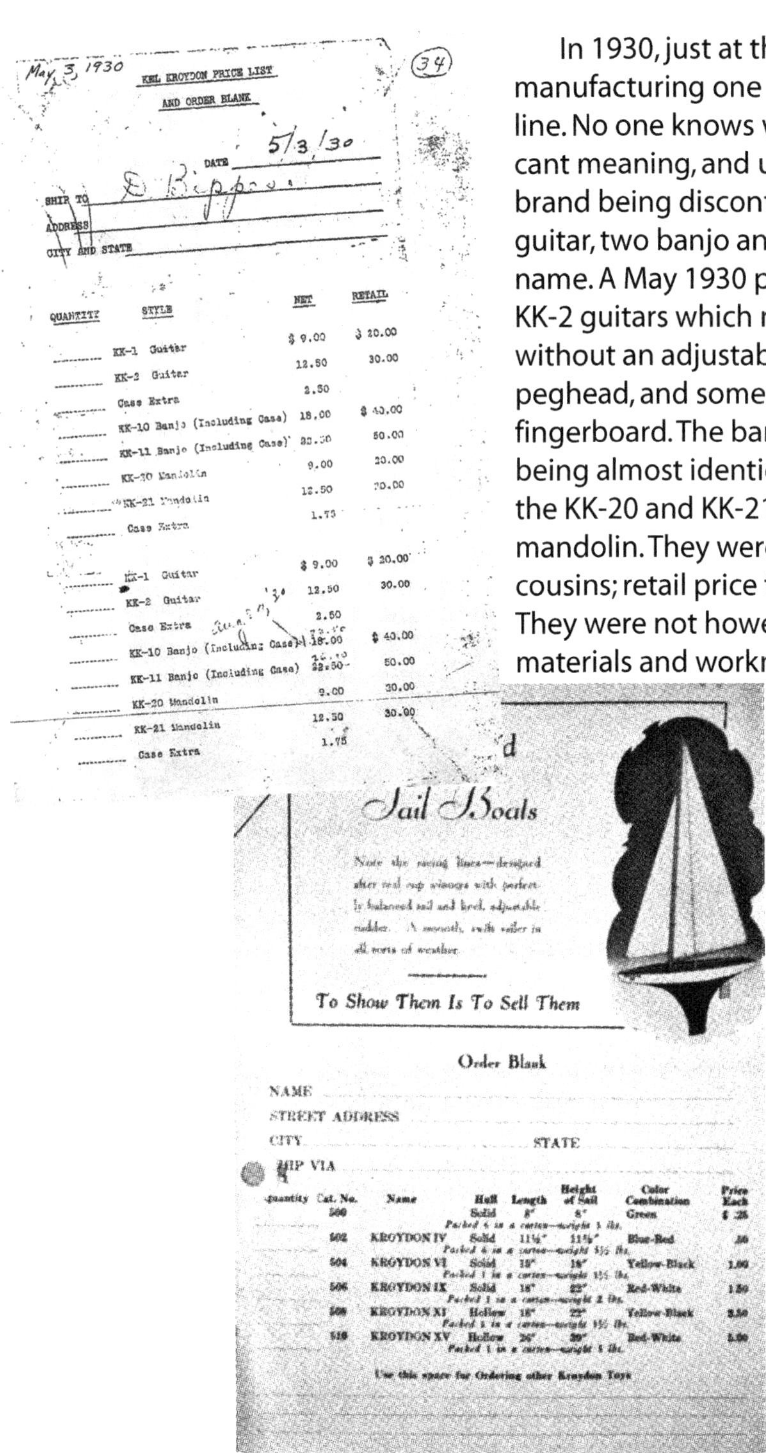

May 3, 1930 (34)

KEL KROYDON PRICE LIST

AND ORDER BLANK

DATE 5/3/30

SHIP TO D. Bippus

ADDRESS

CITY AND STATE

QUANTITY	STYLE	NET	RETAIL
....	KK-1 Guitar	$ 9.00	$ 20.00
....	KK-2 Guitar	12.50	30.00
....	Case Extra	2.50	
....	KK-10 Banjo (Including Case)	18.00	$ 40.00
....	KK-11 Banjo (Including Case)	22.50	50.00
....	KK-20 Mandolin	9.00	20.00
....	KK-21 Mandolin	12.50	30.00
....	Case Extra	1.75	
....	KK-1 Guitar	$ 9.00	$ 20.00
....	KK-2 Guitar	12.50	30.00
....	Case Extra	2.50	
....	KK-10 Banjo (Including Case)	18.00	$ 40.00
....	KK-11 Banjo (Including Case)	22.50	50.00
....	KK-20 Mandolin	9.00	30.00
....	KK-21 Mandolin	12.50	30.00
....	Case Extra	1.75	

Sail Boats

Note the racing lines—designed after real cup winners with perfectly balanced sail and keel, adjustable rudder. A smooth, swift sailer in all sorts of weather.

To Show Them Is To Sell Them

Order Blank

NAME

STREET ADDRESS

CITY STATE

SHIP VIA

Quantity	Cat. No.	Name	Hull	Length	Height of Sail	Color Combination	Price Each
	500		Solid	8"	8"	Green	$ .25
		Packed 6 in a carton—weight 3 lbs.					
	502	KROYDON IV	Solid	11½"	11½"	Blue-Red	.50
		Packed 6 in a carton—weight 5½ lbs.					
	504	KROYDON VI	Solid	15"	18"	Yellow-Black	1.00
		Packed 1 in a carton—weight 1½ lbs.					
	506	KROYDON IX	Solid	18"	22"	Red-White	1.50
		Packed 1 in a carton—weight 2 lbs.					
	508	KROYDON XI	Hollow	18"	22"	Yellow-Black	3.50
		Packed 1 in a carton—weight 1½ lbs.					
	510	KROYDON XV	Hollow	26"	30"	Red-White	5.00
		Packed 1 in a carton—weight 5 lbs.					

Use this space for Ordering other Kroydon Toys

KEL KROYDON COMPANY

In 1930, just at the start of the Great Depression, Gibson started manufacturing one of the first of its non-Gibson brands, the Kel Kroydon line. No one knows where this name came from, or if it had any significant meaning, and unfortunately, would prove to be a fairly short-lived brand being discontinued by 1932. Gibson began marketing two guitar, two banjo and two mandolin models using the Kel Kroydon name. A May 1930 price list and order form included Models: KK-1 and KK-2 guitars which resembled the Gibson flat-top guitar model L-2, but without an adjustable truss rod, a reddish/orange stenciled logo on the peghead, and some even had tropical scenes painted on the body and fingerboard. The banjo models were the KK-10 and KK-11, the later being almost identical to the Gibson TB-11. The price list also includes the KK-20 and KK-21 mandolins, very similar to the Gibson 'A' series mandolin. They were priced at a fraction of the cost of their Gibson cousins; retail price for the KK-1 was $20.00 vs. $75.00 for the Gibson L-2. They were not however "cheap" by comparison in terms of quality of materials and workmanship. All of the Kel Kroydon instruments are highly sought after by collectors, as they are considered to be some of the best instruments Gibson ever produced. In fact, they are also fairly rare and difficult to find in good condition.

Shortly after producing the Kel Kroydon fretted instruments, Gibson's General Manager, Guy Hart decided to start manufacturing a line of wooden model sailboats also using the Kel Kroydon name. They included a scale-model of the America's Cup winner "The Enterprise" and five other models of various sizes and designs. Most historians agree that this venture was Hart's desire to keep the Gibson work force employed due to the effects of the Great Depression and badly sagging instrument sales. Gibson even set up a separate workshop just for toy production, as they added more and more toys under the Kalamazoo Playthings brand. (also see Kalamazoo Chapter 7)

Kel Kroydon Models:

KK-1 Flattop Guitar - 1930-1932
Body: 14 ¾" x 19 ¼"
(similar to Gibson L-00, but no truss rod)
Natural top with two large tropical birds stenciled in color on either side of bridge
Some with natural top & tropical birds design
Dark brown back, sides and neck
Flat-topped peghead shape with
Kel Kroydon red (orange) stenciled logo

KK-2 Flattop Guitar - 1930-1932
Same construction as KK-1
White pearloid veneer peghead and fingerboard with geometric black and orange-stenciled decorations
Large tropical volcano scene or birds stenciled in color on the top
Flat-topped peghead shape with Kel Kroydon
red (orange) stenciled logo

Photos courtesy of Tony Klassen

KK-10 Banjo - 1930-1932 (lower left)
Similar to Gibson TB-11 4-string tenor banjo, but no adjustable truss rod
White pearloid veneer on peghead, fingerboard and back of resonator
Stenciled black designs, no shading, black finished neck, pot and resonator sides.

KK-11 Banjo - 1930-1932 (lower right)
Same basic construction as KK-10, but two color red and black stenciled designs
Blue finish on neck, pot and resonator sides, edges of peghead & back of resonator
A few with orange and black stenciling and brown finish and shading

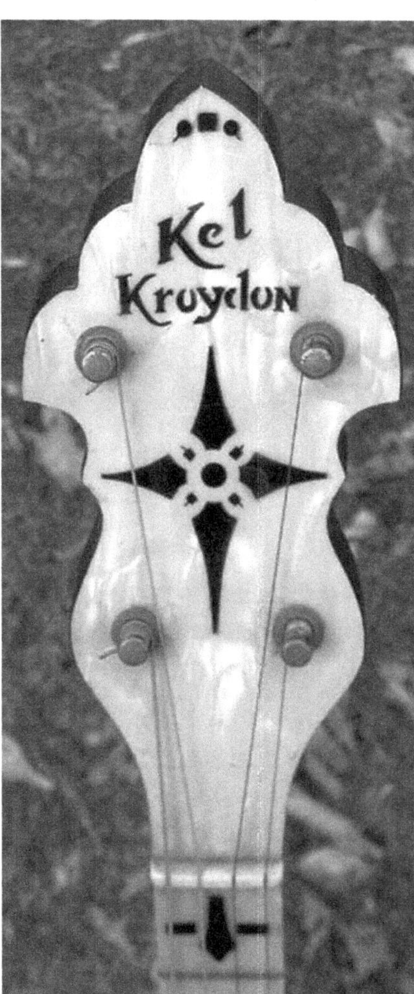

KK-20 Mandolin - 1930-1932
(Similar to the Gibson A style body - no truss rod)
Natural spruce top with oval sound hole & 3 small SH rings
Green shaded sides, back, and neck
Single bound top & NO pickguard
4-on-a-plate tuners with black buttons
Rosewood fingerboard & narrow non-adjustable bridge
Nickel "cloud-shaped" tailpiece

KK-21 Mandolin - 1930-1932 (not pictured)
NO EXAMPLES KNOWN TO EXIST
(Only appears on 1930 Gibson Price List)
Probably same body as KK-20, but with white
pearloid veneer on peghead, fingerboard
Tropical stenciled designs

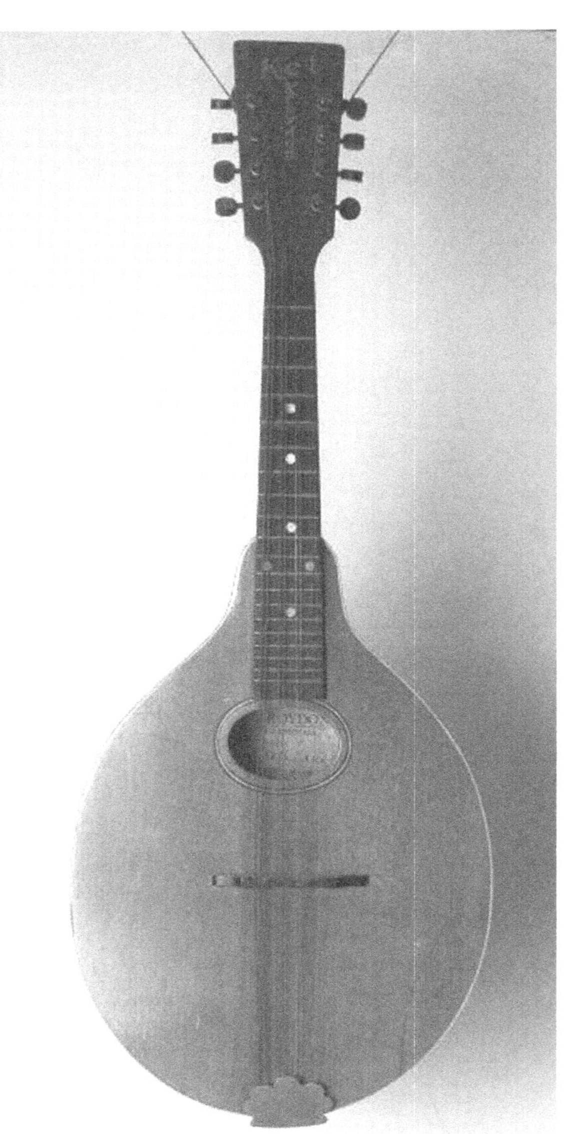

Marshall Special - 1930

Gibson made the "Marshall Special" flattop Hawaiian guitar brand for Lilian G. Marshall, a Hawaiian guitar teacher in Hartford, CT and the director of the Aloha Hawaiian Orchestra. There was only one model guitar Gibson made around 1930-1931 and it was very similar to the Kel Kroydon Model KK-2, complete with the pearloid fingerboard and peghead veneer, stenciled geometric designs and the infamous "volcano" landscape painted on the top. It is considered one of the rarest Gibson-made guitars as only two known examples exist anywhere!

MRS. LILIAN G. MARSHALL
TEACHER OF
HAWAIIAN GUITAR
MANDOLIN - UKULELE
DIRECTOR OF ALOHA HAWAIIAN ORCHESTRA
78 EAST BRANFORD ST. HARTFORD, CONN.

Sold to
Mary Andrews Dec 10, '30

1 Marshall Special Guitar @ $35.00
1 Guitar Case @ 9.25
$44.25

Received payment
Lilian G. Marshall

Dec 10, '30.

A 1930 sales receipt for the Marshall Special guitar.

Guitar Model:

Body size: 14 ¾" x 19 ¼"
Similar to Kel Kroydon KK-2
Flat-topped peghead with stenciled
"Marshal Special" logo
Tropical scenes with volcanoes stenciled on body
Red & black stenciled design on fingerboard
Mahogany back, sides & 12-fret neck
Adirondack red spruce top

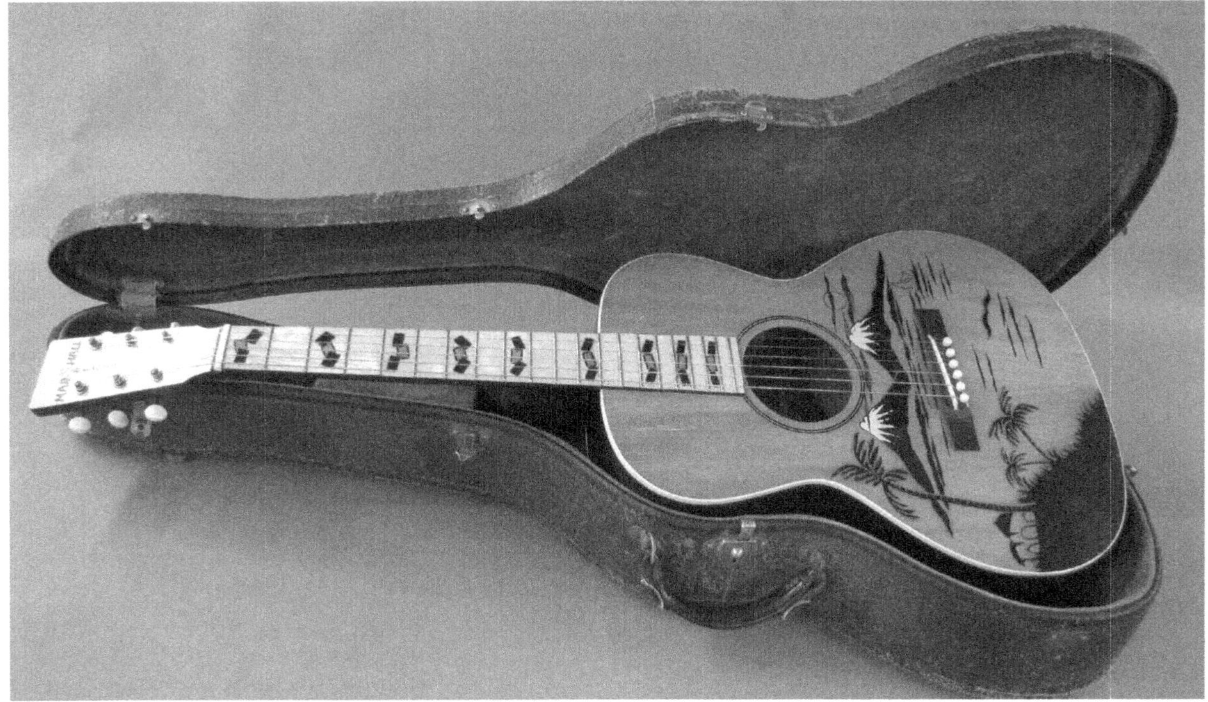

Photos courtesy of Neil Reck

Martelle - 1934

An extremely rare Gibson-made "private label" brand was manufactured for the Kalamazoo Musical Instrument Company's co-owner Charles Martelle. There are only two known models that were produced in 1934 for Martelle and only one or two surviving examples of each model. The Martelle Deluxe was essentially a Gibson Roy Smeck Stage Deluxe with the Martelle name silk-screened on the peghead. The basic design, body size, and appointments vary little from the Smeck. The Martelle Deluxe Custom was probably a "one-off" custom made guitar especially for Charles Martelle himself. It has the same size body as the Gibson "Jumbo", but with a very special pearloid fingerboard and headstock veneer. Only one known example exists.

Martelle Deluxe - Jumbo Flattop Guitar - 1934
(Similar to the Gibson Roy Smeck Stage Deluxe)
Jumbo body 16" x 20 ¼" x 4 ½" deep
12-fret wide Hawaiian-style neck
"Martelle Deluxe" stenciled logo on the peg head
Dark mahogany back, sides & neck - sunburst spruce top

Martelle Deluxe "Custom" - Jumbo Flattop Guitar - 1934
(Shown in gallery section)
Same jumbo body as the Martelle Deluxe
14-fret neck version with "Ivoroid" FB & peghead veneer
"Martelle Deluxe" stenciled logo on the peg head
Elevated tortoise-shell pickguard
Rounded "Crown-top" custom peghead shape
Light sunburst spruce top
(probably a "1-off" custom version made for
Charles Martelle himself)

Photo courtesy of Folkway Music

Mastertone Special - 1939-1942

Gibson used the name "Mastertone" for everything from their top-of-the-line banjos starting in the 1920s to their in-house magazine. They also produced another of their own "house brands" using the "Mastertone" name for low-end Hawaiian style flat-top guitars, lap steels & an electric version of the Kalamazoo KG-11. These guitars were manufactured at the lowest cost possible and produced in vast quantities, sometimes in batches exceeding 150 instruments. Many of the batches were grouped with other models such as the Kalamazoo KG-11s, which had the same basic design. This proved to be very advantageous to Gibson as they were able to manufacture larger batches of bodies and necks, all stamped with the same FON (or batch number), and then divided into the various brands, depending on current orders and/or inventory. The Mastertones were certainly not of the highest quality, but Gibson sold hundreds to various music stores as an inexpensive "beginner" or "student" model that nicely complimented their Spanish and Hawaiian guitar method books.

Mastertone Special - Hawaiian Flat-top guitar
Same body as Kalamazoo KG-11
Flat-topped peghead with
stenciled "Mastertone Special" logo
All mahogany - top, back, sides & neck
3-on-plate tuners with black buttons
(Also available as a square-neck version)

MEHG - Mastertone Electric Hawaiian Guitar
Lap steel similar to Kalamazoo KEH
"Ivoroid" fingerboard with stenciled position markers
Single bound "cream" top, back & FB
Single bar-type pickup with "boomerang" cover plate
1 volume & 1 tone - side jack
"Dark tan ripple spun finish"

MESG - Mastertone Electric Spanish Guitar
Same body as Kalamazoo KG-11
Large round sound hole pickup
Side-mounted jack

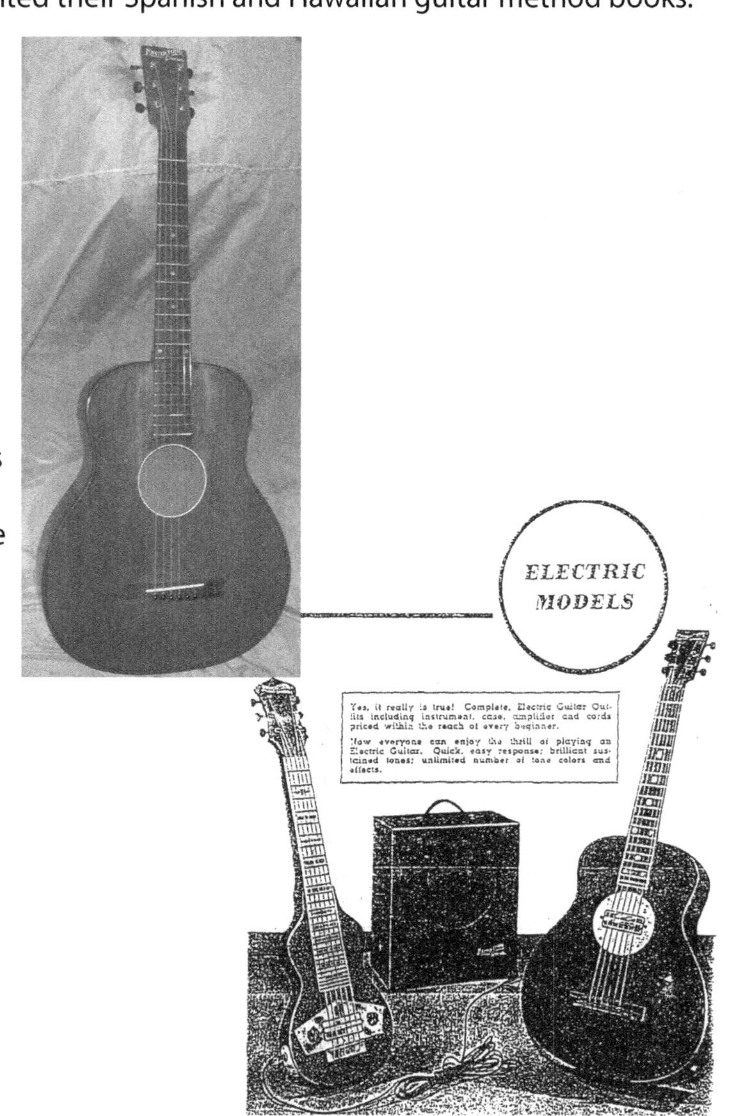

Montgomery Ward - 1929-1940

The Montgomery Ward Company was the world's first great mail order retail company. Aaron Montgomery Ward founded it in Chicago in 1872. Ward had worked for a dry-goods company that would later become Marshall Field & Co, and wanted to establish an easier way to market merchandise to more rural areas. Their first catalog was issued in 1874 and was 32 pages long, but by 1876 in quickly grew to 152 pages and listed 3,000 items. The catalogs included everything from clothing, house-wares, farm equipment, and even windmills. By 1897, Wards boasted sales of $7 million a year and their catalog was nearly 1,000 pages long. In 1926, Wards opened its first retail stores, ushering in a new era that would help them compete with their main rival Sears, Roebuck & Co. By the beginning of the Great Depression, Wards operated more than 500 stores nationwide, which helped sales grow to $600 million by the early 1940s. Wards also operated eight main distribution centers to support their mail order sales division in Chicago (headquarters), Kansas City, MO, Albany, NY, Baltimore, MD, Oakland, CA, Denver, CO, St. Paul, MN and Portland, OR.

Gibson started making instruments for the Montgomery Ward catalog as early as the fall of 1929, and the relationship between the two companies would prove to be the longest and most successful line of "private labeled" instruments lasting until 1940. There was a total of six different brands Gibson made for Montgomery Ward, including the most popular and well-known brand "Recording King". The others were Studio King, Mitchell Brothers, Charles McNeil, Carson Robison and Roy Smeck. The first Gibson-made instrument was the rather expensive "Recording King" Tenor Banjo Model 505, with a price tag of $142.00! It was roughly equivalent to Gibson's Model TB-6, which was one of their more expensive models, as well. The first guitar Gibson made for Wards was the Model 807 "Recording King", an almost exact replica of Gibson's legendary "Nick Lucas Special", but Ward's version was all-black and was sold for the bargain price of $48.00 as compared to $125.00 for the a Gibson NLS. Gibson also supplied the Model 507 a tenor banjo of exceptional quality including gold-plated hardware. The higher-priced Gibson-made instruments wouldn't last long as the Great Depression forced Gibson and Wards to offer lower-priced instruments starting in 1932. Like other "budget brands", Gibson was able to cut the manufacturing costs by eliminating their "patented" adjustable truss rod, which indicates that the process used to install them was rather costly. Most of the other design features did not vary greatly from existing Gibson and other "budget brand" models, enabling Gibson to make use of the same manufacturing processes that were already in place.

Gibson would go on to make many different instruments for Ward's catalogs including guitars, mandolins and banjos. While other manufacturers like Kay and Regal also made many of Ward's instruments, the Gibson-made models were always the most expensive and of the highest quality. Gibson started making instruments for Wards Fall/Winter 1929-1930 catalog, which indicates that the deal was brought about by Frank Campbell, Gibson's sales & marketing manager from January 1925 to December 1931. Campbell, who was also responsible for bringing the Nick Lucas Special to life, probably had a lot to do with starting the Kel Kroydon line, as well as S.S. Stewart, Marshall Special and other early brands, but there's very little information to support this supposition. However, Wards' 1932 Spring/Summer catalog only had one Gibson-made banjo model and Fall/Winter 1932-1933 had no Gibson-made instruments at all. It wasn't until the Spring/Summer 1933 catalog that Wards introduced any new Gibson-made models suggesting that the relationship between the two companies was left in limbo, until Gibson named a successor to Frank Campbell.

In 1932-1933, Neil Abrams of Gibson, Inc. took over the role of managing the "budget brand" instruments in terms of models, pricing, and the relationship with their customers. In the case of Montgomery Ward, many of the Gibson-made models changed from year to year, and many like the Models 507, 682, 807 & 1027/1028 were only made for a brief time making them extremely rare and collectable. Gibson also employed a dual model numbering system (an in-house model # and Ward's catalog model # were often different). Ward did not always list instruments in their catalogs by the same name Gibson used making it difficult to identify a particular model or year. For example, Gibson used the "Tone Crest" brand name, but Wards didn't use the name for their catalog. Gibson also did not want the fact that they were making these guitars for Ward known to the general public, so Montgomery Ward used phrases like "Famous Instruments - By Celebrated Maker".

Wards also had Gibson manufacture "artist endorsed" models with their names as the brand such as Carson Robison, The Mitchell Brothers, Andy Sannella, Charles McNeil, Roy Smeck, and Ray Whitley. These particular brands are among the most recognizable instruments Wards ever carried, as well as making them more valuable to collectors. Although Gibson made in excess of 350 Recording King - Ray Whitley guitars, they are considered to be rare and very collectable, often fetching sums in excess of $15,000.

Montgomery Ward Guitar Models:

Model 681 Recording King Flattop Guitar - 1934-1935
Body 14 ¾" x 19 ¼" (same as Kalamazoo KG-14)
Maple back & sides, spruce top
14-fret Mahogany neck with bound Brazilian RW fingerboard Elevated celluloid pickguard
Single bound top & back
Adjustable bridge (ebony saddle) & nickel extension tailpiece
Nickel 3-on-plate tuners with white buttons

Model 682 Andy Sannella Hawaiian Guitar - 1934-1935
Body 16" x 20 ¼" "Jumbo" Size (same as Gibson J-35)
Mahogany back, sides & 12-fret neck - spruce top
Rosewood fingerboard & bridge with white pins
High bone nut & saddle for Hawaiian playing
Top, back & sound hole bound in white Pyralin

Model 807 Recording King Flattop Guitar - 1930-1931
Body: 14 ¾" x 19 ¼" x 4 5/8" deep
(same as Gibson Nick Lucas Special)
No adjustable truss rod
Mahogany back, sides & 12-fret neck - spruce top
RW fingerboard w/ fancy inlays of different shapes
Engraved mother-of-pearl "Recording King" logo
Finished in "black ebony"

Easy Payments
On Any Musical Instrument Costing $20 or More
SEE PAGE 337
"Recording King" Guitar
"Studio King" Tenor Banjo
By Nationally Known Maker

Model 811 Recording King Flattop Guitar - 1931-1932
Same as the Model 807 except Sunburst top
(same as Gibson Nick Lucas Special)
No adjustable truss rod

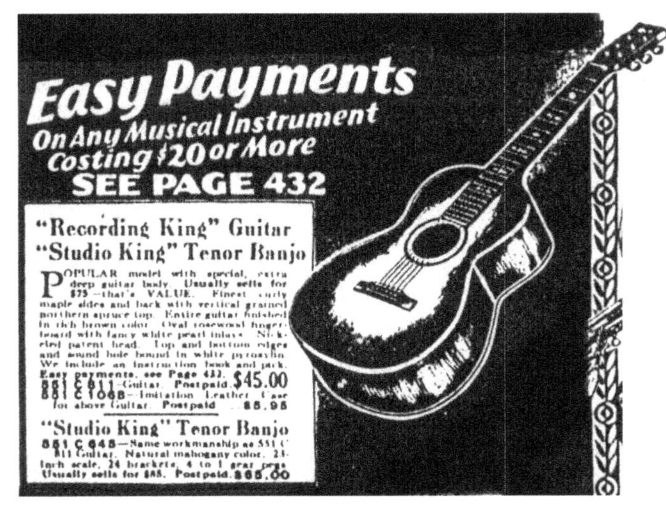

Model 853 Recording King Archtop Guitar - 1934-1935
Small body size 14 ¾" x 17 ½"
Curly maple back & sides
Carved spruce top
14-fret mahogany neck
RW Fingerboard with MOP dots
Adjustable height bridge & nickel extension tailpiece
Single bound top, back & elevated celluloid pickguard

Model 926 "Carson Robison" Flattop Guitar - 1934-1935
Smaller body size 14 ¾" x 17 ½"
Mahogany back, sides & 14-fret neck
Single bound Top, back & sound hole
RW Fingerboard with MOP dots &
RW bridge w/ black pins
Finish: Reddish brown back & sides, small sunburst top

Model 1005 RK Elec. Hawaiian Guitar - 1939-1940
6-string lap-steel guitar - 22 ½" scale length
Small & narrow tear-drop maple body
Maple 12-fret neck w/ RW fingerboard
Single bar-type oval pickup with oval cover plate
1-volume & 1-tone control
Single bound top & back
"Pointed dome" peghead with crown above RK logo
Dark mahogany back, sides & neck - sunburst top

Model 1020 RK Elec. Hawaiian Guitar - 1939-1940
6-string lap-steel guitar - 22 ½" scale length
Larger teardrop maple body
Maple 12-fret neck w/ RW fingerboard
Single bar-type oval pickup with square cover plate
1-volume & 1-tone control
Single bound top & back
"Pointed dome" peghead with crown above RK logo
Dark mahogany back, sides & neck - sunburst top

Model 1023 "Roy Smeck" Guitar Outfit - 1939-1940
#1023 guitar packaged with #1022 amplifier
6-string lap-steel guitar - 22 ½" scale length
Larger guitar-shaped maple body
Maple 12-fret neck w/ RW fingerboard - MOP dots
Single bar-type oval pickup - top-mounted in bridge position NO cover plate
1-volume & 1-tone control
Single bound top, back & fingerboard
"Pointed dome" peghead with crown above RK logo
Dark mahogany back, sides & neck - sunburst top

Model 1127 "Roy Smeck" Electric Spanish - 1938-1940
#1127 guitar only - (#1128 packaged with amplifier)
Full-sized 16 ¼" x 20 ¼" arch-top guitar body
Maple veneer back & sides, spruce top
Mahogany 14-fret neck with RW FB & MOP dots
Single bound top & back, fingerboard & elevated tortoise pickguard (PG notched for pickup)
Single bar-type oval pickup, mounted in neck position
1-volume & 1-tone control above bass-side f-hole
"Pointed dome" peghead shape with MOP RK logo
RW adjustable bridge, nickel trapeze tailpiece
Brown mahogany back, sides & neck - sunburst top

Pictured from left to right: Models 1005, 1020, 1023 & 1127

Model 1027 Recording King "Ray Whitley" Jumbo Flat-top Guitar - 1939-1940
Body 16" x 20 ¼" 'Jumbo' Size (same as Gibson J-35)
Rosewood back & sides - spruce top
Rosewood fingerboard w/ MOP dots
RW 'bat wing' style bridge with white pins
5-ply maple 14-fret neck
Large 'fire stripe" pickguard (similar to Gibson SJ)
Single bound top, back & FB 3-ring sound hole rosette
"Pointed dome" peghead shape with
engraved inlaid MOP RK logo
Natural finish with sunburst top

Model 1028 Recording King "Ray Whitley"
Jumbo Guitar - 1939-1940
Same as Model 1027 except: Mahogany back & sides
14-fret mahogany neck "reinforced with steel rod"
Standard rectangle RW bridge w/ black pins
MOP fingerboard dots

Ray Whitley Jumbo Model

$29.95 Cash — $3 Down, $5 a Month See Page 871

This big Ray Whitley Jumbo Size sells in most places for $80.

Flat Top and Back — Deep, throaty tones . . . just right for voice accompaniments.

Finest Wood — Rosewood back and sides. Eastern Spruce top. Natural Rosewood finish with sunburst on top. Rosewood fingerboard celluloid bound, with Mother-of-Pearl inlaid position markers. 5-ply Maple neck. White celluloid bound top and back edges and fingerboard. Rosewood bridge. Decorated celluloid guard plate. Vertical peghead; nickel plated individual machine heads. Hooks for cord. Size 40⅝ by 16 in. Roberts Instruction Book, 3 guitar Solos, silk Cord and Pick. Shipping weight 13 pounds.

551 B 1027—Cash Price **$29.95**
Time Payments: $3 Dn., $5 a Mo. **32.65**
551 B 1312—Black Keratol Case. Cotton flannel lined. Ship. wt. 13 lbs.. **$4.75**

Best, Jumbo Model

Maker's $37.50 Quality — **$19.95** Cash — $3 a Month See Page 899

Because he finds that the *wider, deeper* body gives *fuller tones*, just right for accompaniments, Ray Whitley endorses the Jumbo.

Flat Top and Back—professional type.
Mahogany back and sides finished in dark Red color. Spruce top with sunburst shading. Rubbed by hand to high gloss. Mahogany neck reinforced with steel rod to prevent warping. Oval celluloid bound Rosewood fingerboard with inlaid Mother of Pearl markers. Cream celluloid bound top and back edges. Rosewood bridge. Celluloid guard plate. Vertical type peghead. Hooks on end of body for cord. SIZE: 41 by 16 in. 4½ in. deep.

We include Allen's Instruction Book, Pick and Silk Cord. Ship. wt. 14 lbs.

551 A 1028—Cash.................. **$19.95**

551 A 1312—Black Keratol covered, Cotton flannel lined, side-opening Case for above. Ship. wt. 13 lbs $4.75

Model 1052 Carson Robison Flat-top Guitar - 1940
Body size 16 ¼" x 20 ¼" (similar to Washburn 5241)
Mahogany back, sides & neck, spruce top
RW fingerboard & bridge (cat. says Braz. RW)
MOP dots at 5th, 7th, 9th, 12th frets
Glued on celluloid pickguard
Dark brown B&S & sunburst top
Single bound top, back & sound hole
"roof-peak" peghead shape with crown RK logo
Carson J Robison "signature" below logo

Model 'K' #1115 Carson Robison Flat-top Guitar
1938-1939
Body size 14 ¾" x 19 ¼" (same as Kalamazoo KG-14)
Mahogany back, sides & neck, spruce top
RW fingerboard & bridge (cat. says Brazilian RW)
MOP dots at 5th, 7th, 9th, 12th frets
Glued on "fire stripe" pickguard
Dark brown B&S & sunburst top
Single bound top, back & sound hole
"Pointed dome" peghead shape with crown RK logo
Carson J Robison "signature" logo below

Model 1135 - "Carson Robison" 3/4 size guitar
1938-1939
Small body Small body 12 ¾"W x 17 ¼" long
Mahogany back, sides & neck - spruce top
RW fingerboard w/ MOP dots up to 12th fret
RW rectangular bridge with white pins
Glued on "fire stripe" pickguard
"Pointed dome" peghead shape RK & CR logos
Dark brown back, sides & neck - sunburst top

Model 1281 "Carson Robison"
Flattop Guitar - 1936-1937
Same as Model 1115
listed above

Model 1136 RK M-2 Archtop Guitar - 1938-1940
Body size 16 ¼" x 20 ¼" (same as Gibson L-50)
Maple veneer back & sides, carved spruce top
RW FB with MOP dot inlays, RW adjustable bridge
"Pointed dome" PH with engraved MOP RIK logo
Single bound "cream" top & back
Bound fingerboard & elevated pickguard
Hinged nickel tailpiece, tuners with black buttons
Red mahogany with "golden" sunburst finish

Model 1137 RK M-3 Archtop Guitar - 1938-1940
Same body as M-2 - Curly maple veneer back & sides
Carved spruce top RW FB with MOP dots
RW adjustable bridge, 5-ply maple 14-fret neck
"Pointed dome" peghead with engraved RK logo
Single bound top & back, FB & elevated pickguard
Hinged nickel tailpiece & individual tuners
Red mahogany with "golden" sunburst finish

Model 1123 RK M-4 Archtop Guitar - 1938-1940
Body size 16 ¼" x 20 ¼" (similar to Gibson L-50)
Curly maple veneer back & sides
Carved spruce top, RW FB with "oval" inlays
RW adjustable bridge
5-ply maple 14-fret neck
"Pointed dome" peghead with engraved RK logo
Single bound "cream" top & back, FB & pickguard
Hinged nickel tailpiece & individual tuners
Chocolate brown & "beige" sunburst finish

Model 1124 RK M-5 Archtop Guitar - 1938-1940
Body size 16 ¼" x 20 ¼" by 4 ½" deep
Curly maple back & sides, Carved spruce top
RW fingerboard with large "diamond" MOP inlays
RW adjustable bridge w/ MOP "diamond" inlays on sides
5-ply maple 14-fret neck
"Pointed dome" peghead with crown & RK logo
"Checkered" binding, brown & amber sunburst finish

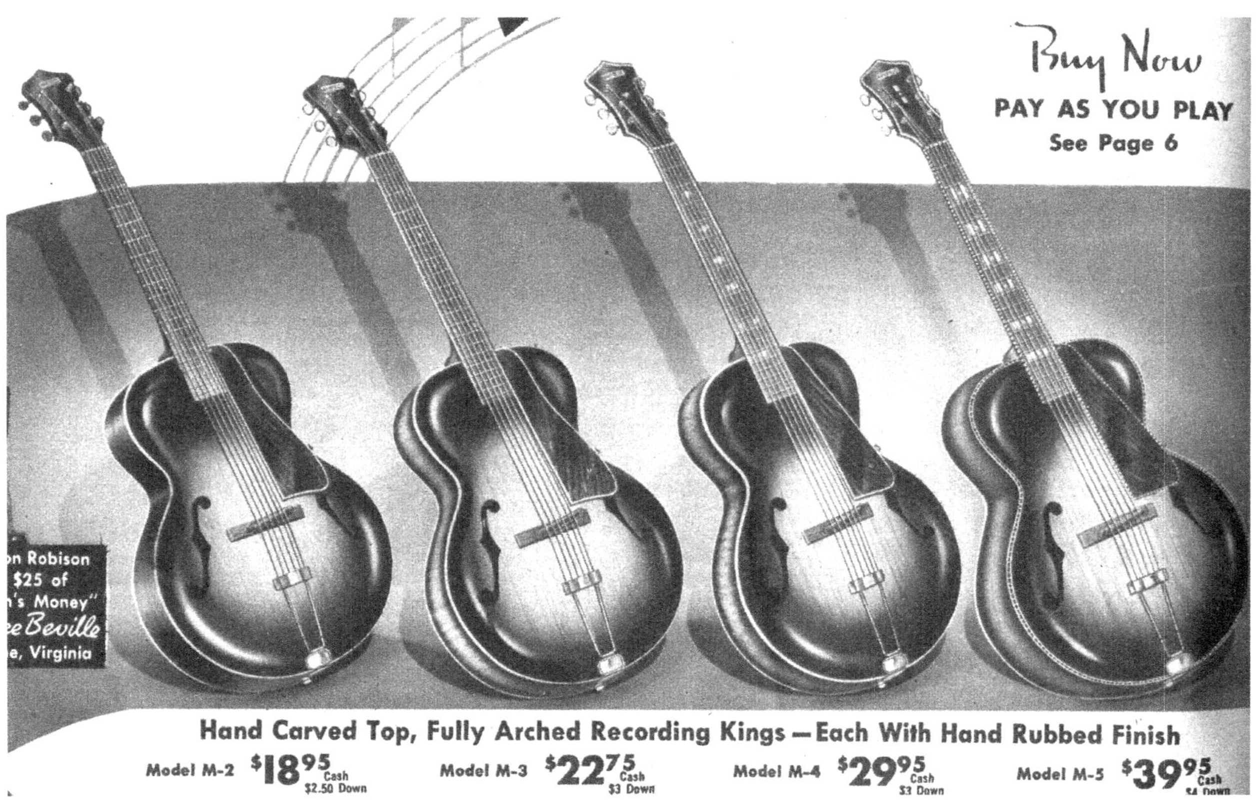

Model 1129/1151 Recording King "Roy Smeck" Electric Hawaiian Guitar - 1938-1940
#1151 guitar only (#1129 packaged with amplifier)
6-string lap-steel guitar - 22 ½" scale length
Small pear-shaped maple body
Maple 12-fret neck w/ RW fingerboard
Single bar-type oval pickup - top-mounted in bridge position NO cover plate
1-volume & 1-tone control
Dark mahogany back, sides & neck - sunburst top

Model 1139 Recording King Electric Hawaiian Guitar - 1938-1939
Packaged with #1139 amplifier w/ 8" speaker
6-string Lap-steel guitar
Small rectangular-shaped brown maple body
Maple 12-fret neck w/ RW fingerboard
Single bar-type pickup with large rectangular cover plate
1-volume & 1-tone control

Maple Hawaiian Guitar Outfit

- Rich Brown Maple Body
- Chromium Plated Cover
- Usual $75 Value—Save $25

$49.95 Model A

New electric amplifying Guitar Outfit, constructed to give the best performance at a low price. Maple neck; Rosewood fingerboard with 22½-inch scale. Volume and tone control on top. Complete with Amplifier that can be used for 2 instruments. Made of wood, covered with heavy airsheen material. 3 stages amplification, 110–120 volts, A.C. 50 to 60 cycles. 4 tubes. 8-inch heavy duty dynamic speaker. Slipover cover, Alvino Ray instruction book included. Ship. wt. outfit 41 lbs.

351 C 1139—Hawaiian Guitar Outfit.$49.95
351 C 1140—Mahogany Spanish Guitar Outfit. Super Auditorium size. Complete with amplifier described above. Ship. wt. 39 lbs.$49.95
As low as $5 down for each above. See Page 6.

Roy Smeck Electric Amplifyi

$65.00 Model A-104 With Amplifier Save $39

Hawaiian Guitar Outfit: Usual $104 value. Dark Mahogany finished Maple body. Celluloid bound top edge. Standard 22½-in. scale. Rosewood fingerboard with 24 inlaid frets; Mother-of-pearl position dots. Volume and tone controls on top. Grover individual machine heads. Ultra-sensitive pickup. Complete with Amplifier described below and Alvino Ray instruction book.

351 C 1129—Outfit. Wt. 41 lbs. $65.00
551 C 1151—Guitar only. Wt. 15 lbs. 29.95
Buy on Time Payments—See Page 6

Amplifier included with above guitars: Hig
Black artificial leather. 3 stages amplification wit
50–60 cycles. 5 standard tubes; 10-inch Jensen spe
and a microphone. 10-foot cord. On-and-off switch.
551 C 1149—Amplifier Only with water proof sl

Model 1282 "Tone Crest" Arch-top Guitar - 1936-1937
This model only listed on internal Gibson memo,
but did not appear in a Ward's catalog (see Model 1283)

Model 1283 "Tone Crest" Arch-top Guitar - 1936-1937
Gibson referred to Models 1282 & 1283 as "Tone Crest",
but not called by that name in Ward's catalog
Body size 16" x 20 ¼" (similar to Gibson L-50)
Veneer maple back & sides
Non-carved "arched" spruce top
14-fret mahogany neck
RW Fingerboard with MOP dots
Adjustable height bridge & nickel extension tailpiece
Single bound "cream" top, back, and fingerboard
Elevated "cream" celluloid pickguard
Natural varnish finish

April 10, 1936

INSTRUMENTS FOR MONTGOMERY WARD & COMPANY
FALL AND WINTER CATALOG
(1936-37)

CATALOG NO.	NAME	NET PRICE TO WARDS
#1281	Carson Robison Guitar	5.75
#1282	Tone Crest Guitar	9.35
#1283	Tone Crest Guitar	10.70
#1284	Recording King Guitar	17.00
#1285	Recording King Guitar	21.39
#1642	Recording King Mandolin	8.75
#1593	Recording King Banjo	14.00

The string numbers and prices will not be changed, and will be continued as in last catalog.

Right: A 1936 Gibson pricing memo for the "Tone Crest" brand guitars

Customer after Customer Tell Us
"WARDS ARCHED TOP and BACK GUITARS
Have the Deeper Tone and Greater Volume of Guitars up to $35"

Centuries of expert craftsmanship have proved that arched top and back construction produces finer tone than flat guitars. Scientifically arched, durably constructed, fully braced against possible warping, their tone will please the discerning professional player and inspire the student. *Hand rubbed piano polish finish.*

Natural Curly Maple Super Auditorium Size

- Usual $35 Value
- Highly figured Northern hard curly maple back and sides
- Fine Eastern Spruce top

Product of America's most famous maker. Arched top and back assures greater strength and more power. Shell celluloid bound. Naturally finished with several coats of clear varnish to preserve the beautiful figure in the wood. Brazilian Rosewood oval fingerboard bound with cream celluloid. Honduras mahogany neck. Rosewood adjustable bridge. Size 41½ by 16¼ inches. Complete with Adams Instruction Book, Nick Lucas pick and 12-lesson certificate. Ship. wt. 11 lbs.
551 C 1283..........$19.75
551 C 1392—Case for above. Black Keratol covered, side opening. Flannel lined. Ship. wt. 9 lbs..............$4.10

Model 1284 Recording King Arch-top Guitar - 1936-1937
Very similar to M-2

Model 1285 Recording King Arch-top Guitar - 1936-1937
Very similar to M-5

Own the *Famous Make* Preferred by Stars of Stage and Radio

Wards Save You from 40% to 60%

Hand Carved Top Guitars

The final perfect product of centuries of fine instrument making! Finer than regular arched guitars because the high "violin" arches of these superb instruments are Hand Carved from inch-thick Spruce! Every wood fiber is left free to vibrate perfectly, producing a rich powerful tone that carries through any orchestra combination. Most of all the shaping and *ALL* of the finishing is done *by hand*. Used by all the foremost professional players except those who require the special qualities of an amplifying or electric guitar. Especially fine for radio work because of the unusual richness and clarity of tone.

Professional Model

- Super Auditorium Size
- Beautiful Curly Maple Back and Sides
- Hand Carved and Graduated Spruce Top

(A) Thrill to the beauty and tone of this guitar! Made by America's most famous maker—it usually sells for $50.00. High-lighted mahogany finish with hand shading. Hand rubbed finish. Arched top and back. Honduras mahogany neck reinforced with steel rod. Rosewood oval fingerboard, inlaid pearl position dots. Top and back edges celluloid bound. Polished celluloid finger rest. Grover individual machine heads. Adjustable bridge. Monel metal strings. 41½ by 16¼ in. Adams Guitar Book, pick, 12-lesson certificate.
551 C 1284—Ship. wt. 11 lbs.........$29.95
Monthly Payment Price: $3 Down, $5 a Month.......... 32.95
551 C 1394—Arched Case. Keratol covered, flannel lined for above guitar. Shipping weight 9 pounds..........$5.35

Artist Model

- Super Auditorium Size
- Northern Curly Maple Back and Sides
- Selected Eastern Spruce Top, Hand Carved and Hand Graduated for Brilliant Tone
- Hand Rubbed Mahogany Finish—Golden Sunburst

(B) Only Wards can offer this nationally advertised $100 guitar at this price! Extra deep body gives tonal power for orchestra, radio, etc. Arched top and back. Brazilian Rosewood oval fingerboard. Body and fingerboard checker bound with cream and black celluloid. Rosewood adjustable bridge. Grover individual machine heads. Honduras Mahogany neck reinforced with steel rod. 41½ by 16¼ inches. Adams Guitar Book, pick.
551 C 1285—Ship. wt. 11 lbs.....$39.95
Monthly Payment Price: $4 Down, $5 a Month.......... 43.95
551 C 1395—Arched Case. Keratol covered, flannel lined for above guitar. Ship. wt. 9 lbs..........$5.35

Model 1121/1122 17" RK M-5 Archtop Guitar - 1940
Model 1121 with nickel-plated hardware
Model 1122 with gold-plated hardware
Body size 17" x 20 ¼" by 4 ½" deep
Curly maple back & sides, Carved spruce top
RW fingerboard with large "diamond" MOP inlays
RW bridge w/ MOP "diamond" inlays on sides
5-ply maple 14-fret neck
"Pointed dome" peghead shape with engraved
MOP crown & RK logo with large diamond
Multi-ply binding top, single bound back,
fingerboard & pickguard
Chocolate brown & "Amber" sunburst back, sides, & top

Y ARCHED GUITARS

uditorium size. • Fully arched top and back.
top, carved and graduated by hand.
-finger, oval Rosewood fingerboard. Pearl dots.
inforced with steel rod to prevent warping; joins body
fret. • Celluloid bound shell guard plate.
ble Rosewood bridge. • Nickel plated hinge tailpiece.
type peghead inlaid with Mother of Pearl.

Maker's $100 Quality $39.95 Cash

Recording King Orchestra models with larger bodies for deeper tone. Each string in correct balance with others.
Selected Curly Maple Back and Sides—matched Eastern Spruce top. Hand rubbed Brown Mahogany finish. 5-ply Maple neck. Top and back celluloid bound. Size: 41⅜ by 17 in. 4 in. deep. Terms, Page 899. Shipping weight each 14 pounds.
551 A 1121—Chrome plated parts..$39.95
551 A 1122—Metal parts Gold plated; Back, top hand carved—finer tone $59.95
551 A 1377—Case. Black Keratol covered. Curly plush lined. Ship. wt. 13 lbs.... $11.98

Model 1025 Roy Smeck 8-String Console Steel - 1939-1940
(Model 1024 packaged with amp)
E 9th tuning
Curly maple body Rosewood fingerboard
Mother-of-pearl dots markers
Single pickup

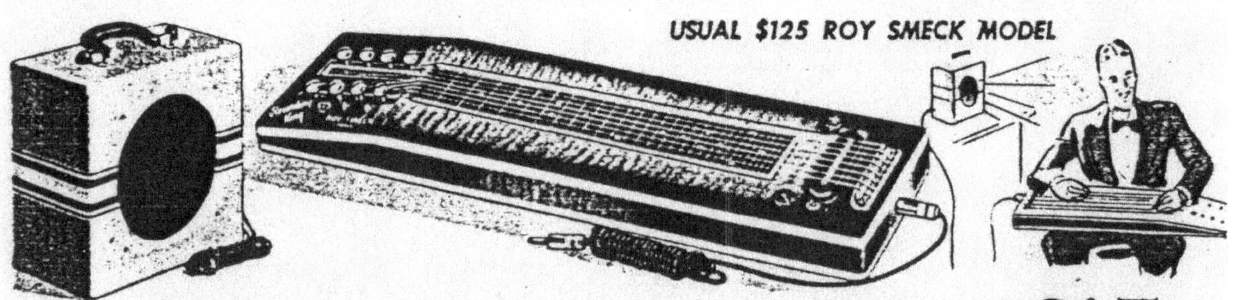

CONSOLE MODEL—8-STRING ELECTRIC HAWAIIAN GUITAR OUTFIT $94.75

Most top-notch guitar artists use Hawaiian Guitars with 8 strings. On this Roy Smeck model, strings are tuned left to right: 8th F♯, 7th E, 6th B, 5th D, 4th E, 3rd G♯, 2nd B, 1st E. Called E 9th tuning. Gives more complete chords, closer harmony, and movement from one chord to another is faster. Terms, Page 1009.

All Curly Maple Body. Rosewood fingerboard, Mother of Pearl dots. Celluloid edges. Magnet pickup. Machine heads easily adjusted. 31¼ x 8⅛ in. x 2 in. 10-ft. cord, amplifier 551 C 1013 above, Instructions.
351 C 1024—Guitar and Amplifier. Wt. 43 lbs. $94.75
551 C 1025—Guitar Only. Ship. wt. 23 lbs... $59.95
551 C 1372—Keratol Carrying Case. Wt. 17 lbs. $9.98

Banjos & Mandolin Models

Model 505 Recording King Tenor Banjo - 1929-1930
Standard 23" scale length (similar to Gibson TB-6)
11" mahogany shell & 13 1/2" resonator
"Nickled" flange & armrest - 24 brackets
"Ivorette" bound FB & peghead
Ebony FB with fancy MOP inlays
Rogers calfskin head
4:1-ratio tuners

Model 507 Recording King Tenor Banjo - 1930-1931
(Pictured at beginning of this chapter)
Standard 23" scale length
Maple Rim & neck
Gold-plated hardware - 24 brackets
Bound RW fingerboard & PH w/ MOP inlay design
Rogers calfskin head
Deluxe 4:1 ratio Grover tuners

Model 641 Studio King Plectrum Banjo - 1929-1930
same as Model 645 with plectrum banjo neck
26" scale length

Model 645 Studio King Tenor Banjo - 1929-1930
Standard 23" scale length (similar to Gibson TB-6)
11" shell & 13 1/2" figured maple arched resonator
Chromium-plated hardware - 24 brackets
"Ivorette" bound FB & peghead
Ebony FB with fancy MOP inlays
Rogers calfskin head
Deluxe 4:1 ratio Grover tuners
Cremona brown sunburst

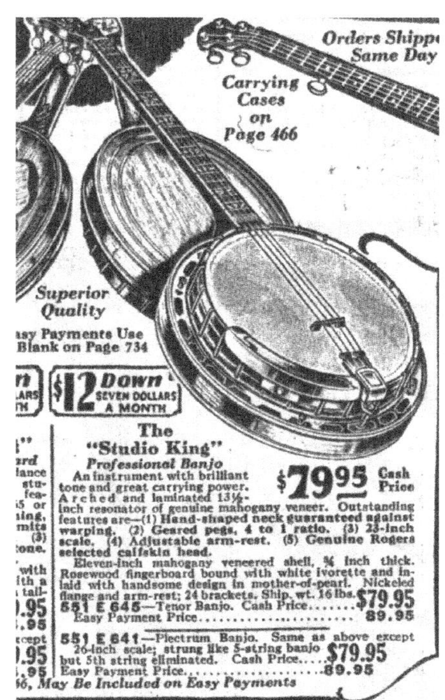

Model 731 Recording King Tenor Banjo - 1934-1935
Same as 732, but with 24 brackets
Mahogany neck & Red Mahogany finish

Model 732 Recording King Tenor Banjo - 1930-1933
23" scale length 4-string tenor banjo
7-ply 11" shell with "Birdseye" maple
13 ½" convex resonator
Flamed maple adjustable neck with steel rod
Brazilian RW fingerboard wit MOP position markers
Nickel-plated resonator flange,
20 brackets, arm rest & tailpiece
Grover tuning pegs, white calfskin head
Amber brown neck & sunburst resonator

Model 1593 Mitchell Brothers Tenor Banjo 1934-1935
Model 1593 changed to Charles McNeil banjo 1936-1940
23" scale length 4-string tenor banjo
3-ply 11" shell with figured maple 13 ¾" resonator
Flamed maple adjustable neck with steel rod
Brazilian RW fingerboard wit MOP position markers
Nickel-plated resonator flange, 24 brackets,
arm rest & tailpiece

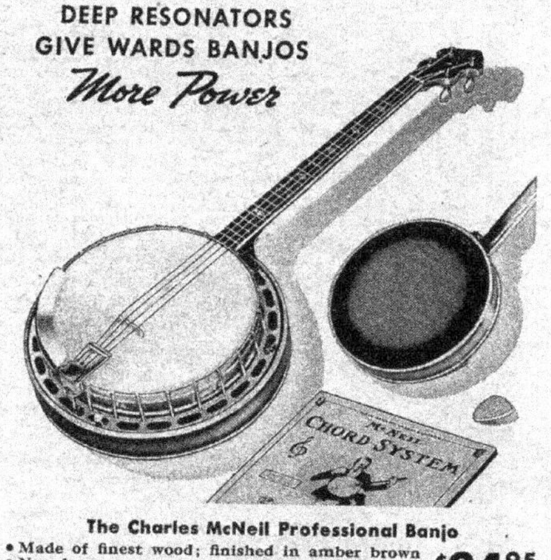

Model 701 Tenor Banjo - 1930-1931
Similar to Gibson TB-11
Heavy laminated 11" shell
13 ½" arched mahogany resonator
23" scale length
Nickel-plated hardware
White pearloid peghead and fingerboard

Model 605 Tenor Banjo - 1930-1931
Same as 701, but with mahogany resonator
(Not shown)

In the Usual $65 Price Class

New Beauty
Pearl and Black Color
Tenor Banjo Outfit

$45.00 Complete

A symphony in color as well as in tone. Picture this beautiful Tenor Banjo with its lustrous white pearl-like ivorette facing that covers resonator, and fingerboard and the contrasting effect of jet black decorations against this shimmering background. Heavy laminated 11-inch shell, 13½-inch professional resonator, arched and acoustically correct. 23-inch scale. Nickel-plated straining hoop, armrest, tailpiece, and resonator flange. 24 nickel-plated professional brackets. Geared non-slipping pegs with white buttons. Elaborately shaped peg head with top facing in white pearl colored ivorette; neck, rim and side of resonator finished in mahogany. Each fret is hand worked to insure accuracy and ease of playing. Complete outfit includes a very sturdily constructed side opening carrying case covered with imitation leather and lined with plush, a quick method instruction book for sel. teaching, pick and set of strings. **We Pay Postage.**

551 G 701— Complete outfit **$45.00**

Genuine Mahogany
Exceptionally fine quality, a grade that usually sells for $100 in most stores. Similar to 551 G 701 but with mahogany shell and resonator; rosewood fingerboard bound with ivorette and inlaid with mother-of-pearl. **Postpaid.**

551 G 605 — Complete outfit........ **$79.85**

For easy payments see Budget Plan on Page 457.

We Pay Postage

Williams Modern Method for Tenor Banjo

Models 952/953 Tenor or 5-string Banjo - 1940
11" Maple plywood shell
Dark Mahogany finish
"Ebonized" maple fingerboard
Nickel-plated hardware

Model 954 Tenor Banjo - 1940
13 ¾" maple resonator
11" maple plywood shell
16 Nickel-plated brackets
Amber-brown sunburst finish

Models 955/956 5-string or Tenor Banjo - 1940
13 ¾" bound maple resonator
11" maple plywood shell
24 Nickel-plated brackets
Amber-brown sunburst finish

Model 957 Tenor Banjo - 1940
13 ¾" bound mahogany resonator
11" solid maple shell
24 Nickel-plated brackets
Dark brown finish

Model 807 Recording King Mandolin - 1934-1935
Gibson A-style mandolin body
Mahogany back & sides, sunburst spruce top
RW fingerboard with MOP dots
Glued on celluloid pickguard
Single bound top only, bound sound hole

Model 969 Mandolin - 1940
Similar to Gibson A-50 (14" scale-length)
Spruce top, curly maple B&S
Mahogany neck with
"ebonized" FB
Celluloid binding &
elevated pickguard
Special Blonde finish

1642 Mandolin - 1936-1937
Carved spruce top with f-holes
Curly maple back & sides
Mahogany neck
Rosewood fingerboard
Elevated celluloid pickguard

1607 Mandolin - 1936
(Not shown)
Same as 1642
Mahogany back & sides

National - 1944 - 1961

From 1944 to 1961, Gibson built guitars for Valco Manufacturing Co., makers of the legendary National resonator guitars. CMI (Chicago Musical Instruments) bought Gibson in early 1944, and also had exclusive distribution rights for National/Valco. These guitars also had the unique distinction of being the only Gibson-made instruments manufactured after WWII, for another company. This was probably due to the CMI connection between both companies, and Valco wanted to expand the National line with new guitar models. Up to about 1949, Gibson made guitar bodies with standard dovetailed wood necks, but without truss rods. After that, National installed their own magnesium-core bolt-on neck called the "Stylist". The neck was held on by one large horizontal bolt and the fingerboard was held down by two screws under the pearl dot markers, which was essentially the same construction as National's pre-war resonator guitars. The idea was to make an "un-warpable" neck and although it made the guitars "neck heavy" they produced an acceptable sound. Gibson continued to make many guitar bodies for National until about 1952, when manufacturing for most of the guitars was taken over by Kay. Gibson did continue to make bodies for the National Model 1155 acoustic guitar and 1155E acoustic/electric guitar, as well as the "Bel-Aire" until 1961. The Del-Mar electric guitar was made by Gibson from 1954 to 1957, but was discontinued in 1958.

A 1947 pre-production sales flyer for the National Aristocrat

National 'Stylist' neck sales brochure cover

In July 1944, Gibson started making "prototype" guitars they shipped to CMI, but were slated to become a new line of National acoustic and electric guitars, and mandolins. The prototypes/samples carried "N" prefix model numbers that roughly corresponded Gibson models, but the letter "N" was substituted for Gibson's L-prefix (i.e. National N-5 = Gibson L-5, N-50 = L-50, etc.). However, there are some other strange and mysterious instruments that do not correspond to Gibson models, like the "N So." which appears to have been a National version of Gibson Southerner Jumbo, and the N-100 which is listed as a 16 1/4" wide arch-top, but does not match up to any Gibson model. Unfortunately, there are few known examples of these guitars and most of the information presented here comes from Gibson's shipping records from Jan. 1944 through Mar. 1947, and one National price list called the "Tentative Postwar List of National Instruments" which dates from 1946. By 1948, Gibson was in full production building guitars for National, and the "N" designation was dropped in favor of new model names and numbers. Example: N-50 became Model 1145, etc. Very few "N prototypes" are known to still exist and are extremely rare and collectable.

Model & Description

B-125 - Unknown model or type
N-100 - No corresponding Gibson model
N-111 - Similar to Gibson's J-100
N-12 - Probably similar to the L-12 archtop
N-125 - Probably similar to the L-7 archtop guitar
N-150 - Probably similar to the L-10 archtop guitar
N-275 - Same size as Gibson 17" L-5
N-275B - Price List says B=natural finish
N-31 - Only mandolin on National Price list and Gibson shipping records (possibly like an A-1)
N-33 - Gibson LG-size guitar (changed to Model 1160)
N-4 - Probably similar to L-4 archtop
N-45 - J-45 Jumbo guitar (changed to Model 1155)
N-5 R - Similar to L-5 archtop R=regular or sunburst finish
N-5 N - Similar to L-5 archtop N=natural finish
N-50 - Similar to the Gibson L-50 archtop
N-66 - Jumbo-sized flat-top, probably similar to the J-55
N-7 - Similar to the L-7
NE-125 - Similar to Gibson ES-125 electric guitar
NE-150 - Similar to Gibson ES-150 electric guitar
NE-300 - Similar to Gibson ES-300 electric guitar
NM-00 - Similar to Gibson A-00 mandolin
NM-50 - Similar to Gibson A-50 mandolin
N.S. - Unknown model - case #515 indicates it was same size a Gibson 16 ¼" wide archtop
N So. - Believed to be a National version of Gibson's Southerner Jumbo (same case # as N-45/J-45)

NATIONAL

Tentative Postwar List of National Instruments, Amplifiers and Cases.

This list includes familiar pre-war models plus several new carved and flat-top Spanish guitars and three mandolins. The National line for post-war will include the ever popular diaphragm amplified instruments such as the Collegians, Aragons, Style O's, M-3's and S-3's, which are not shown on this list.

CARVED SPANISH GUITARS AND CASES

No.	Description	Price
No. N-275	Regular Finish, Size 17 x 21	$275.00
No. N-275B	Blonde Finish, Size 17 x 21	285.00
No. 5-D	Case for above	30.00
No. N-150	Regular Finish, Size 17 x 21	150.00
No. N-150B	Blonde Finish, Size 17 x 21	160.00
No. 5-D	Case for above	30.00
No. N-125	Regular Finish, Size 17 x 21	125.00
No. N-125B	Blonde Finish, Size 17 x 21	135.00
No. 5-D	Case for above	30.00
No. N-100	Regular Finish, Size 16¼ x 20¼	95.00
No. N-100B	Blonde Finish, Size 16¼ x 20¼	100.00
No. 5-C	Case for above	25.00
No. N-50	Regular Finish Only, Size 16¼ x 20¼	50.00
No. 4S	Case for above	10.00

SPECIAL ARCHED MODEL SPANISH GUITAR AND CASE

No.	Description	Price
No. NA-35	Regular Finish Only, Size 16¼ x 20 ¼	35.00
	Case for above	7.00

NATIONAL FLAT TOP GUITARS AND CASES

No.	Description	Price
No. N-111	Jumbo, Regular Finish, Size 17 x 21	125.00
	Case for above	25.00
No. N-66	Jumbo, Regular Finish, Size 16 x 20½	60.00
	Case for above	19.00
	Case for above	10.00
No. N-33	Regular Finish, Size 14⅛ x 19¼	35.00
	Case for above	7.50

CARVED MODEL MANDOLINS AND CASES

No.	Description	Price
No. N-51	Regular Finish	50.00
No. N-51B	Blonde Finish	55.00
	Case for above	15.00
	Case for above	6.00
No. N-31	Regular Finish Only	30.00
	Case for above	6.00

NATIONAL ELECTRIC SPANISH GUITARS AND CASES

No.	Description	Price
No. 440	Aristocrat, Regular Finish, Size 17 x 21	$150.00
No. 440B	Aristocrat, Blonde Finish, Size 17 x 21	160.00
	Case for above	30.00
	Case for above	22.50
No. 71	New Yorker, Regular Finish, Size 16¼ x 20¼	100.00
No. 71B	New Yorker, Blonde Finish, Size 16¼ x 20¼	105.00
	Case for above	20.00
	Case for above	10.00
No. 220	Princess, Regular Finish, Size 15 x 19½	75.00
No. 220B	Princess, Blonde Finish, Size 15 x 19½	80.00
	Case for above	20.00
	Case for above	10.00

NATIONAL ELECTRIC HAWAIIAN GUITARS AND CASES

No.	Description	Price
No. 87-O	Waikiki Outfit	98.50
No. 97-O	Waikiki DeLuxe Outfit	139.50
No. 120	Princess Hawaiian Guitar	60.00
No. 5-A	Case for above	15.00
No. 86	Dynamic Hawaiian Guitar	75.00
No. 6-D	Case for above	15.00
No. 70	New Yorker Hawaiian Guitar (6 strings)	90.00
No. 85	New Yorker Hawaiian Guitar (7 strings)	100.00
No. 5-A	Case for above	15.00

NATIONAL AMPLIFIERS

No.	Price
No. 300	75.00
No. 400	105.00
No. 500	125.00

SUBJECT TO PRICES IN EFFECT AT TIME OF SHIPMENT

General information on Logos and Peg head inlays:
Inlaid Mother of Pearl logos on all high-end guitars
Metal: Nickel-plated small shield logo with red and blue enamel: Model 1160
Large metal shield logo with silver, blue & red enamel: Models 1145 & 1155
1947-49: un-plated brass with white enamel
1949-51: Small shield
Plastic/pot metal: Die-cut, thin white plastic script logo, 1155, 1952/55, thick, gold flash-plated pot metal, 1109 and 1198 Bel-Aire, 1155. Some of the last of these logos may be plated plastic instead of pot metal.

Gibson-made National Models:

Model N-111 Acoustic flattop guitar - 1945-1946
Super jumbo body size: 17" x 21"
"Bat wing" style bridge or slight variant
Pearl dot position markers
Triangular pickguard
Sunburst finish

Model N-275 Acoustic arch-top guitar - 1944-1946
Body size: 17" x 21" (same as Gibson L-5)
Flamed maple back & side, spruce top
Triple-split parallelogram inlays
Shield & banner inlaid pearl peghead logo
Elevated tortoise-shell pickguard
Triple-bound pearl/tortoise/pearl throughout
Sunburst finish

Model 1135 Acoustic arch-top guitar - 1947-1953
Previously Model N-150 - 1944-1946
Body size: 17"x 21" (same as the Gibson L-7)
With Gibson-made neck - 1947-1951
With National "Stylist" neck - 1951-1953
Split half-circle fingerboard inlays
Triple-bound top & single bound FB & peghead
Blonde or sunburst finish
Discontinued in 1953

Model 1145 Acoustic arch-top guitar - 1947-1951
Body size: 16: x 20 ¼" (same as Gibson L-50)
Replaced by a Kay-made body in 1951
Dot fingerboard inlays
Elevated celluloid pickguard
Sunburst finish

Model 1155 Acoustic Flat-top Guitar - 1947-1952
Similar to the Gibson J-45
'Jumbo' size body 16" x 20 ¼"
Mahogany back & sides - spruce top
Rosewood fingerboard w/ MOP dots
RW 'pointed rectangle' style bridge with white pins
14-fret neck, Sunburst top finish
No truss rod

Model 1155E Acoustic/Electric Guitar - 1954-1957
Same as 1155 with internal pickup
1-volume & 1-tone knob mounted on upper bout

Model 1160 Acoustic Flat-top Guitar - 1947 - 1951
Similar to the Gibson LG-3
Replaced by a Kay-made body in 1951
Body size 14 1/8" x 19 ¼"
Mahogany back & sides - spruce top
Rosewood fingerboard w/ MOP dots
Square-bottom "tear drop" pickguard

Model 1110 "Aristocrat" Electric Guitar - 1947 - 1951
Body size: 17" x 21" (same as Gibson ES-300)
With Gibson-made neck - 1947-1951
With National "Stylist" neck - 1951-1953
Triple-split parallelogram inlays
Clear pickguard
1-neck pickup & 1-"bridge tone" PU
1-"Touch-Tone" volume & tone w/"chicken-head" knob
Triple-bound top, back, fingerboard & peghead
Sunburst finish

Model 1109 "Bel-Aire" Electric Guitar - 1948-1959
(See 1957 catalog page below)
Body size: 16 1/4" x 20 1/4" (same as Gibson ES-175)
Top-mounted 1-neck & 1-bridge pickup
Top-mounted 1-volume, 1-tone & PU selector
Controls: 2-way lever PU selector switch
(front PU, back PU, both Pus) 3-volume knobs
above strings (front, back & both); big knob by
treble f-hole is master TONE, not volume.
Single sharp cutaway
Butterfly FB inlays & peghead
Sunburst finish

Model 1198E "Bel-Aire" Electric Guitar
Same as 1109 with 3 pickups

Model 1103 "Del-Mar" Electric Guitar - 1954-1957
Body size: 17" x 21" (same as Gibson ES-300)
Top-mounted 1-neck & 1-bridge pickup
Top-mounted 1-volume, 1-tone & PU selector
Single rounded cutaway
Butterfly FB inlays & peghead
Sunburst finish

Chapter 14

Old Kraftsman - 1936-1937

Spiegel, Inc, a leading retailer of clothing, apparel, and home furnishings is best known for its namesake, the Spiegel catalog, The Spiegel catalog dates back to 1888 as an extension of a successful home furnishings business started by Joseph Spiegel in Chicago, IL. Son, Arthur Spiegel entered the business in 1903 with plans to develop the mail order operations. In 1905, Spiegel was the first mail-order business to offer customers purchasing on credit and as they began to offer installment plans through the mail they used slogans like "No Money Needed", "Many Months To Pay" and especially, "We Trust the People - Everywhere!" Like Montgomery Ward and Sears, Spiegel wanted to target rural areas outside of Chicago that did not have access to retail stores. The company's sales soared to $1 million by 1906 and was renamed Spiegel, May, Stern and Company, with Arthur Spiegel as the president Arthur Spiegel was also an early investor in another new industry, motion pictures. Arthur Spiegel provided the investment backing to Lewis J. Selznick to start Equitable Films in Fort Lee, NJ, which then merged with World Pictures with Spiegel as President and General manager. To this day, Arthur Spiegel has a star on the Hollywood Walk of Fame.

Although Spiegel had a few retail establishments throughout Chicago by the beginning of the Great Depression, and by 1932 the last Spiegel furniture store in Chicago closed its doors. However, the mail-order business continued to grow in spite of the dire economic conditions and soared to $56 million by 1937.

8708 Old Kraftsman Arch-top Guitar - 1937
(Pictured on page 69 - 2nd from left)
Similar to Recording King M-5
Body size 16 ¼" x 20 ¼" by 4 ½" deep
Curly maple back & sides, Carved spruce top
RW fingerboard with large "diamond" MOP inlays
RW adjustable bridge w/ MOP "diamond" inlays on sides
5-ply maple 14-fret neck
"Pointed dome" peghead shape with engraved MOP crown & RK logo with large diamond
"Checkered" or multi-ply binding top, single bound back, fingerboard & elevated pickguard
Hinged nickel tailpiece & individual Grover tuners

8709 Old Kraftsman Electric Spanish Guitar Outfit - 1937
(Pictured on page 69 - 3rd from left)
Same as Recording King #1127 packaged with amp
Full-sized 16 ¼" x 20 ¼" arch-top guitar body (similar to Gibson ES-150)
Maple veneer back & sides, spruce top
Mahogany 14-fret neck with RW fingerboard & MOP dots
Single bound top & back, fingerboard & elevated tortoise pickguard (PG notched for pickup)
Single bar-type oval pickup - top-mounted in neck position
1-volume & 1-tone control above bass-side f-hole
"Pointed dome" peghead shape with engraved MOP Recording King logo
RW adjustable bridge, nickel trapeze tailpiece
Brown mahogany back, sides & neck - sunburst top

8710 Electric. Hawaiian Guitar Outfit - 1937
(Pictured on page 69 - on right)
Same as Recording King #1023 guitar packaged with #1022 amplifier)
6-string lap-steel guitar - 22 ½" scale length
Larger guitar-shaped maple body
Wide maple 12-fret neck w/ RW fingerboard - MOP dots
Single bar-type oval pickup - top-mounted in bridge position NO cover plate
1-volume & 1-tone control
Single bound top, back & fingerboard
"Pointed dome" peghead shape with Old Kraftsman logo
Dark mahogany back, sides & neck - sunburst top

8713 Amplifier
(Pictured on page 69 - on right)
Also see Chapter 19

Guitars . . Endorsed by Professionals

Electric Models

Old Kraftsman—Hand-Carved

$29.95 with case

Standard list price $50! A favorite of radio stars! Auditorium size. Genuine hand-carved top of selected Spruce—Curly Maple back and sides with hand-rubbed and polished finish shading from glowing Amber to rich dark Brown. Arched back gives richer tone qualities and greater volume.

Oval fingerboard for fast professional playing; adjustable rosewood bridge; Cream celluloid bound edges, fingerboard and finger rest. New improved patent heads.

Complete, Including: Brown waterproof carrying case, silk neck cord and 3 gold leaf initials. Please state initials.

RJ8707. *Old Kraftsman* Outfit. **$29.95**

Old Kraftsman Registered Supreme

$44.95 with case

Super Grand Auditorium Size. Individually registered for your protection. For professionals who want only the best!

Its superb tone and volume, its unusual beauty and costly construction features make it easily worth $75! Hand-carved top of eastern Spruce; Curly Maple back and sides finished in shades of Brown, hand-rubbed and polished. Oval fingerboard and head with mother-of-pearl inlay. Adjustable bridge; celluloid binding.

Complete, Including: Keratol-covered carrying case, silk neck cord and 3 gold leaf initials. Please state initials.

RJ8708. Registered Supreme.... **$44.95**

Electric Amplifying Kay Kraft

$69.95 complete

Every string individually amplified—4 times the volume of a single guitar. Spanish model can be used with or without the amplifier. **Amplifier**—5-tube with 10-inch dynamic speaker and volume control. Can be used with 2 instruments and microphone. Operates on 110 volts, 50 to 60 cycles A.C. **Guitar**—super grand auditorium size, with arched top and back on Spanish model; hand-carved top; adjustable bridge and oval fingerboard. Neck cord and 3 gold leaf initials. Please state initials.

RJ8709. (A) Spanish Outfit and Amplifier........ **$69.95**
RJ8710. (B) Hawaiian Outfit and Amplifier....... 69.95
RJ8713. 5-Tube Amplifying Unit Only........... 44.95

Keratol-Covered Waterproof Carrying Cases

RJ8711. For Spanish Guitar...................... **$3.95**
RJ8712. For Hawaiian Guitar..................... 1.95

Microphone for Vocal Amplification

RJ8714. With 25-ft. cord, adjustable stand........ **$17.95**

Consult the Handy Index on Pages 357 and 358 for Your Other Needs

Spiegel's 293

Old Kraftsman Guitar Models:

2154 Old Kraftsman Arch-top Guitar - 1936
Body size 16 ¼" x 20 ¼" (same as Gibson L-50)
Curly maple veneer back & sides - spruce top
RW fingerboard and adjustable bridge
Mahogany 14-fret neck - 25.4" scale length
"Pointed dome" shaped peghead with fancy scroll design & Old Kraftsman logo
Single bound top & back
Bound elevated celluloid pickguard
Nickel tuners & trapeze tailpiece
Mahogany finish with sunburst shaded back, sides & top

8707 Old Kraftsman Arch-top Guitar - 1937
(Pictured on page 69)
Same as #2154, but model number changed for Spring/Summer 1937 catalog

OLD KRAFTSMAN Guitar Outfit

Nationally famous Spanish guitar—sells for $40.00 elsewhere! Played and recommended by such stars as Hoyt "Slim" Bryant and Jack Dunigan pictured above. Selected hard curly Maple auditorium size body with Eastern Spruce top; Rosewood fingerboard and bridge; Mahogany head. Arched top and back—like expensive violins. Hand-rubbed Mahogany finish with white celluloid bound edges. Oval fingerboard for fast professional playing. Complete with Brown Leatherette case, silk neck cord and 3 gold leaf initials. Please state initials.
PJ2154. No Money Down............$29.95

Chapter 15

S.S. Stewart - 1931-1932

Samuel Swain Stewart established the S. S. Stewart Company in Philadelphia, PA in the 1870s. Previous to this time, Stewart had also run a music store in Philadelphia, but set up his own shop to manufacture banjos under the S.S. Stewart and Acme brand names. The Acme banjos were sold by Sears, Roebuck & Co., while the Stewart brand was sold directly to the public. After Stewart's untimely death in 1898, his partner, George Bauer, continued to manufacture banjos using the S.S. Stewart name. In 1915, the S.S. Stewart brand name was purchased by New York-based musical instrument distributor Buegeleisen & Jacobson, who had other companies like William Lange/Paramount handle the manufacturing of the banjos. Around 1931, Buegeleisen & Jacobson had Gibson build one guitar and one banjo model with the S.S. Stewart brand. Gibson produced many banjos similar to its Style 11 under the name Kel Kroydon, but a much smaller number under the name S. S. Stewart. The basic hardware of the banjo model was identical to Gibson's TB-11, as was the fingerboard. However, the peghead had a different shape than the Gibson with the S. S. Stewart name inlaid in mother-of-pearl. The guitar model was nearly identical to the Gibson L-2 flattop guitar, including the same exact body size, neck, elevated pick-guard and natural finish. Only a couple of examples of the Gibson-made S.S. Stewart guitar still exist making it extremely rare and very collectable.

S. S. Stewart Professional Guitars

Orchestra Model

No. A15. S. S. STEWART. Orchestra Model. **Grand Concert Size.** Body made of selected mahogany; selected spruce top; satin finish; both edges and sound hole bound with broad white celluloid and inlaid with thin lines of black and white. Raised celluloid guardplate screwed on side of guitar. Rosewood bridge with bone saddle; white bridge pins.

Neck made of genuine mahogany, with oval rosewood fingerboard and 7 inlaid pearl positions. Bound with white celluloid and inlaid with thin lines of black and white on sides. 6 black side positions. Rosewood veneered head inlaid with name S. S. STEWART and fancy design in pearl. Nickel-plated machines set into metal bushed holes.

This instrument has been designed for the professional who requires a guitar of fine tonal quality. The construction and material used are of the highest quality, yet it is moderately priced. The finish and tone are equal to many guitars being sold at a considerably higher price...**Each $35.00**

No. A415. **S. S. STEWART Orchestra Model Tenor Guitar. Grand Concert** Size body, full professional scale; otherwise the same general make-up as No. A15 Guitar. **Each $35.00**

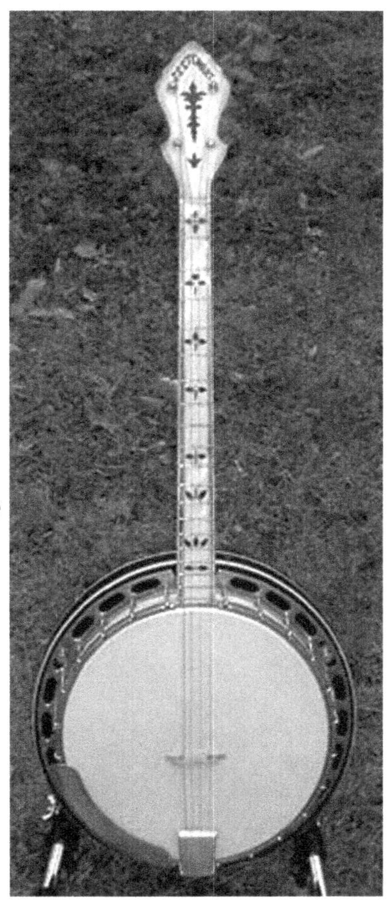

Tonk Brothers - Fascinator - 1935-1936

The Tonk Brothers carried another in-house brand called "Fascinator" and most of these instruments were made by Regal and the Harmony company starting in the early 1930's. For a brief period of time from 1935 to early 1936, Gibson manufactured three Fascinator brand guitars and one mandolin. They were fairly expensive instruments, which might explain their short-lived production run. The Fascinators were pretty much re-labeled Cromwells except Gibson eliminated the "skunk stripe" down the middle of the fingerboard and added two additional mother-of-pearl position markers at the twelfth fret on the archtop models. The flattop guitar model 4960 only had the position markers at the fifth, seventh, ninth & twelfth frets. It is likely that Gibson made very few of the Fascinator instruments as there are no known surviving instruments.

Fascinator Models:

4960 Flat-top acoustic guitar
Body size: 14 ¾" x 19 ¼" (same as Gibson L-00)
Maple back & sides, spruce top
14-fret mahogany neck
RW fingerboard & bridge
Larger MOP dots at 5th, 7th & 9th frets
Smaller double dot at 12th fret
Single-bound top & back
Sunburst finish

display photo Facinator 9 to
Tonk Bros.

4-5284 Tonk Bros

4980 - Arch-top acoustic guitar - Body size: same as 4970
Mahogany back & sides, carved spruce top; Bound RW fingerboard & RW adjustable bridge
Single-bound triangular pickguard; Triple-bound top, single-bound back
Varied pattern MOP FB inlays with 3-piece cross pattern FB inlay at 3rd fret
V-shaped peghead inlay with small diamond; 3-on-a-plate tuners, nickel trapeze tailpiece

Fascinator Guitars

Beautiful to the eye and lovely to the ear completely expresses the qualities of these modern styled instruments which have endeared themselves to musicians and music lovers everywhere.

Their handsome appearance and rich vibrant tone are a high tribute to the quality materials and expert craftsmanship employed in their creation.

Guitar-Grand Auditorium Size

Specifications—Style 4980

This model as illustrated is made with arched top and back. Neither time nor expense have been spared in perfecting this instrument. The top is actually carved out of a piece of Eastern spruce 1" thick and hand graduated to insure fine tonal quality and full volume. Back, side, and neck are of finest grade Honduras mahogany. The rim is deeper than on ordinary guitars and the back is scientifically arched to conform with the carved top. The neck is artistically shaped and reinforced with a steel rod.

Both edges, finger board, and peg head are handsomely bound with cream colored celluloid. Exceptional care has been used on the genuine rosewood fingerboard to insure light and accurate action. Equipped with finest fittings, such as Grover Individual Machines, adjustable rosewood bridge, extension tailpiece, fine finger-rest. The fine tone and exquisite finish of this instrument belies its modest price.

Each **$85.00**

4970 Arch-top acoustic guitar
Body size: 16 1/4"x 20 ¼" (same as Gibson L-50)
Mahogany back & sides, arched spruce top
Brazilian RW fingerboard & adjustable bridge
Single-bound triangular pickguard
Triple-bound top, single-bound back
3 FB dots at the 12th fret, single dots all others
3-on-a-plate tuners, nickel trapeze tailpiece

5284 Mandolin
Body same as Gibson A-style mandolin
Arched spruce top with f-holes
Mahogany back & sides
RW fingerboard & adjustable height bridge
Single-bound top & back
"Clam-shell" tailpiece cover
Elevated tortoise-shell pickguard
Sunburst finish

All Fascinator illustrations courtesy of the National Music Museum

Tonk Brothers - Washburn - 1938-1940

This Chicago based manufacturer originally started as the Tonk manufacturing company (patent). The four Tonk brothers were William, Charles, Albert, and Max who established Tonk brothers as manufacturers of pianos and piano supplies. Later on the firm separated into a music publishing business in New York and piano manufacturing in Chicago. The Washburn brand dates back to the late 1800s when George "Washburn" Lyon was one of the founders of Lyon & Healy Company of Chicago. In 1928, L&H ceased manufacturing their own instruments and the Tonk Brothers took over manufacturing the Washburn brand. From the late 1920s until 1940, several other manufacturers like Regal and Kay made Washburns, except for a brief two-year period from 1938-1940,. There was significant management shake-up at Regal that left the Tonk Brothers without a manufacturer for the Washburn guitars, so they rekindled their previous relationship with Gibson to produce guitars and mandolins with the Washburn name. The model names like "Aristocrat" and "Classic" were the same model names Tonk started using in the late 1920's, but the designs had changed including 14-fret necks and Gibson-style body sizes.

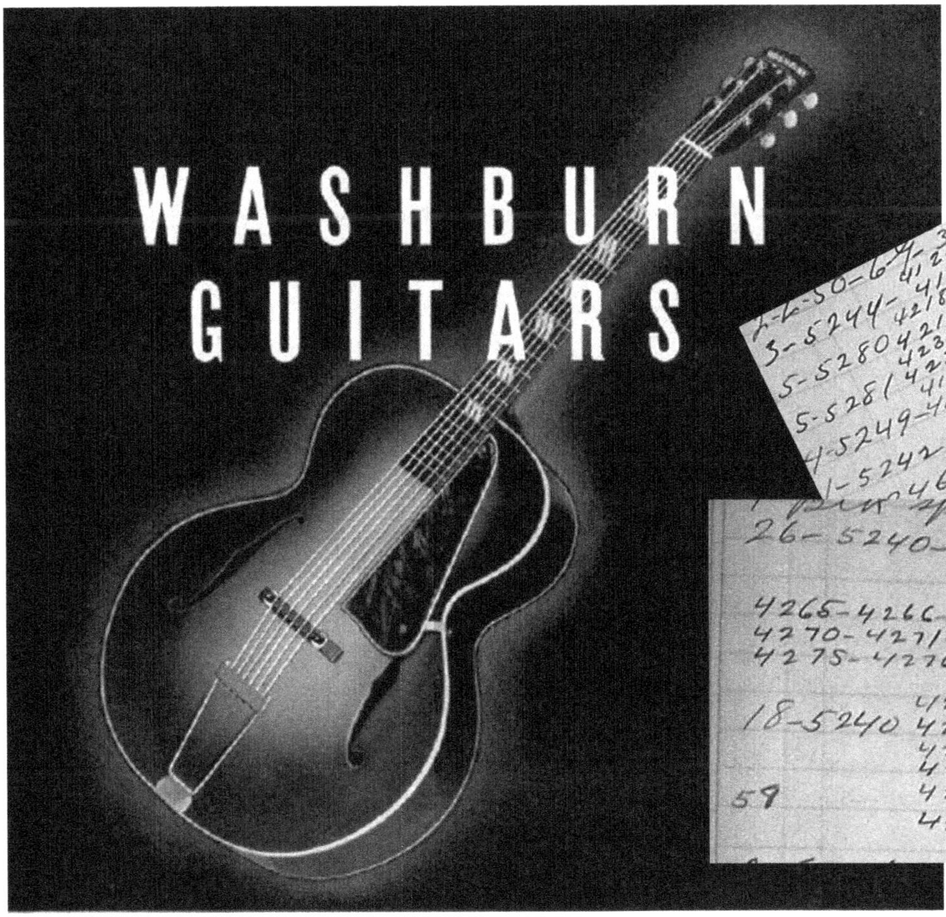

WASHBURN GUITARS

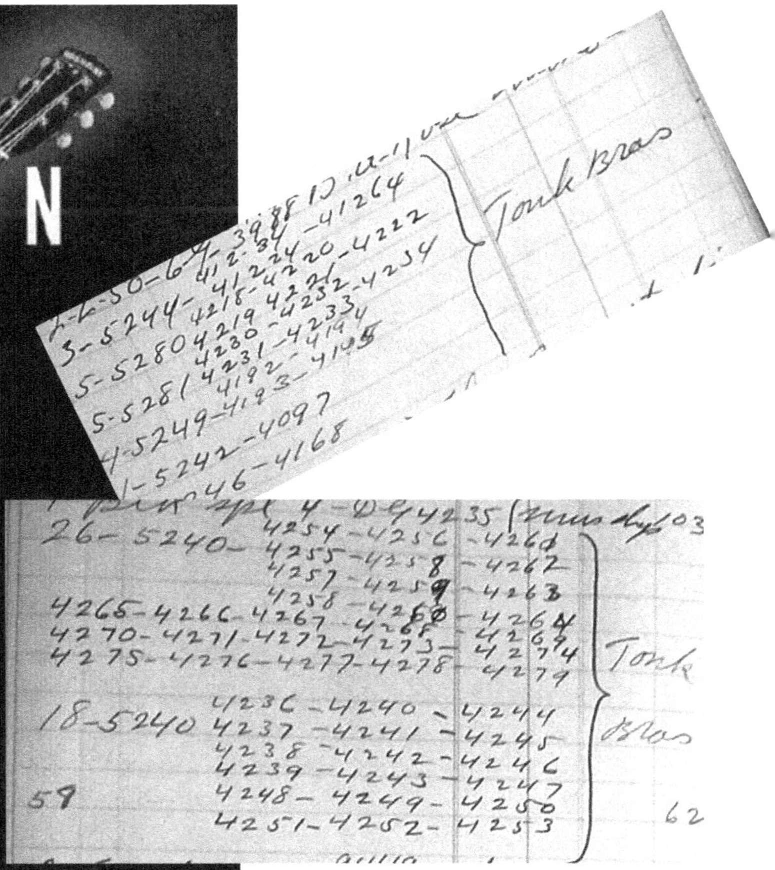

Guitar Models:

5240 Junior - Flattop guitar
Same as Kalamazoo KG-11 with sunburst top
Fancy striped celluloid PH design with slanted "Washburn" logo
Rounded "Martin" style fire stripe pickguard
NO binding except PH & sound hole

5241 Classic - Flattop guitar
Body: 16 ¼" x 20 ¼" (unusual arch-top size w/ flat-top)
Mahogany back, sides & 14-fret neck - spruce top
RW fingerboard & pin bridge
Fancy striped celluloid PH design with slanted "Washburn" logo
Single bound "cream" top, FB & sound hole
All natural finish

"Junior" Model
No. 5240

"Classic Model"
No. 5241

5242 Collegian - Archtop guitar
Same body as Kalamazoo KG-31
Mahogany sides, and laminated back
Arched spruce top
14-fret mahogany neck
RW fingerboard with dot MOP inlays
Adjustable RW bridge and nickel trapeze tailpiece
Single bound top & back
Elevated tortoise shell pickguard
Sunburst top, natural sides and back

"Collegian" Model
No. 5242

5243 Aristocrat - Archtop guitar
Same body size as 5241, but arched top & back
(similar to RK M-3)
Mahogany sides, and laminated or pressed back
Carved spruce top
14-fret mahogany neck
RW fingerboard with parallelogram-shaped MOP inlays
Adjustable RW bridge and nickel trapeze tailpiece
Single bound top & back, FB, and
elevated "tortoise" pickguard
Same peghead shape as 5241, but inlaid MOP logo
Sunburst top, natural sides and back

"Aristocrat" Model
No. 5243

5244 Inspiration - Flattop guitar
15 1/2" "Large Auditorium Size" body
Spruce top, mahogany back & sides
5-ply maple & mahogany neck with
steel reinforcing rod (not truss rod)
Ebony fingerboard & bridge
14-fret neck
Single bound top & back
Small "tear drop" tortoise pickguard

5246 Solo - Flattop guitar (not shown)
15 1/2" "Large Auditorium Size" body
X-braced spruce top
Mahogany back & sides
14-fret 5-ply mahogany neck with steel rod
RW peg head with MOP inlaid Washburn logo
Ebony FB & pin bridge with curved ends
Natural finish

"Inspiration" Model
No. 5244

"Solo" Model
No. 5246

5248 Superb
Similar to 1124 RK M-5
Ebony board with triple parallelogram inlays
Single bound top and back
B&W checkered pickguard binding
5-ply neck mahogany neck with
steel reinforcing rod (not truss rod)
Sunburst top and back

5249 Solo Deluxe
Same body as 5246 Solo
RW back & sides
5-ply neck mahogany neck with
steel reinforcing rod (not truss rod)
Bound FB with large block inlays
Ebony Washburn-style "smile" bridge
Vertical logo on PH with extra pearl inlay
Sunburst finish

"Superb" Model
No. 5248

"Solo De Luxe" Model
No. 5249

5280 Mandolin
Flat-back - Spruce top
Mahogany back, sides & neck
Multi-ply bound top & sound hole
Single bound back & neck
Natural finish

5281 Mandolin
Flat-back - Spruce top
Maple back, sides & "reinforced" neck
Multi-ply bound top & sound hole
Single bound back & neck
14" scale length
Natural finish

Trujo - Truett - 1930-1932

The Trujo Banjo Company was founded by husband and wife, Harry H. George and Velma Truett in San Francisco during in the 1920's. The name "Tru-jo" seems to be a contraction of Truett and "Jo" for George. Harry George was originally a studio guitarists turned banjo player who wanted to have his own line of banjos. The "Truett" banjo line was one of the first "private labeled" brands Gibson made for the Trujo starting around 1928. The banjo was highly ornate with a fancy carved peghead design in the shape of a gothic-style face. Gibson also produced one guitar model around 1930-31 called the "Trujo", which was very similar to the Kel Kroydon KK-1, except it had a custom headstock design and used banjo-style tuners. Apparently, the Depression caused Trujo to go out of business around 1932 ending the short run of instruments made by Gibson. Both the Trujo guitar and Truett banjos are extremely rare and are highly collectible.

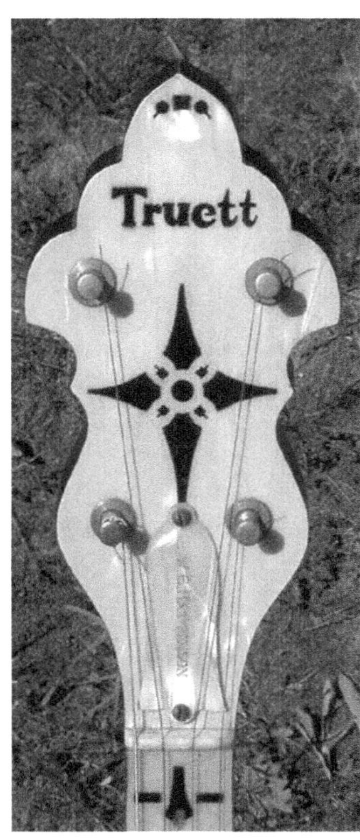

Photo courtesy of Turtlehill Banjos

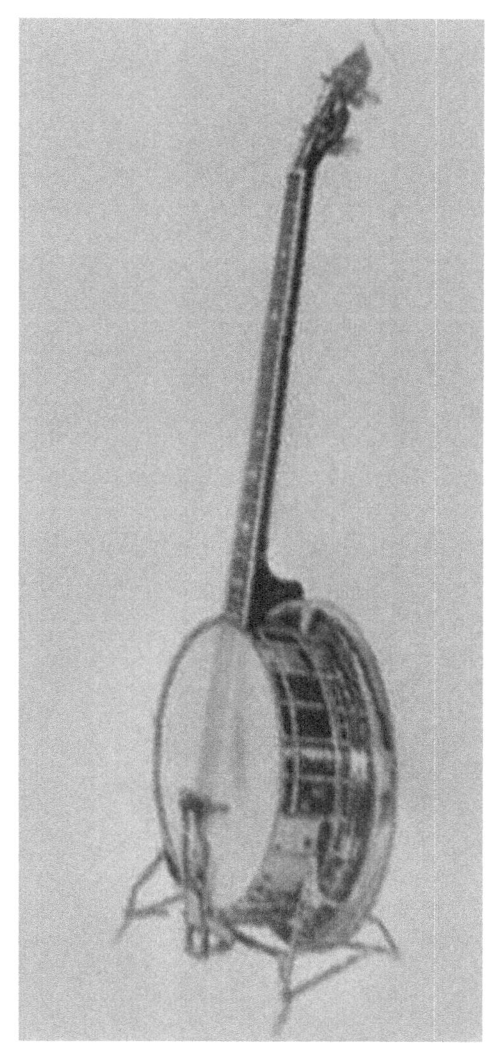

Instrument Models:
Truett Banjo - Style 1 - c1930-1932
Similar to the Kel Kroydon KK-10
White pearloid peghead, FB and back of resonator; Stenciled black designs, no shading,
Black finish on neck, pot & resonator sides
Black stenciled Truett logo

Truett Banjo - Style 2 - c1930-1932
Similar to the Kel Kroydon KK-11
White pearloid veneer on peghead with
Two color red and black stenciled designs
Dark finish on neck, pot & resonator sides
Edges of peghead & back of resonator
Green shading on back of resonator
Black stenciled Truett logo

Trujo Guitar - c1930-1932
Similar to the Kel Kroydon KK-1
Body size 14 ¾" W x 19 ¼" long
Spruce top, RW FB & bridge
Mahogany back, side &
12-fret neck
Carved peghead design,
MOP with engraved Trujo logo
Banjo-style tuners

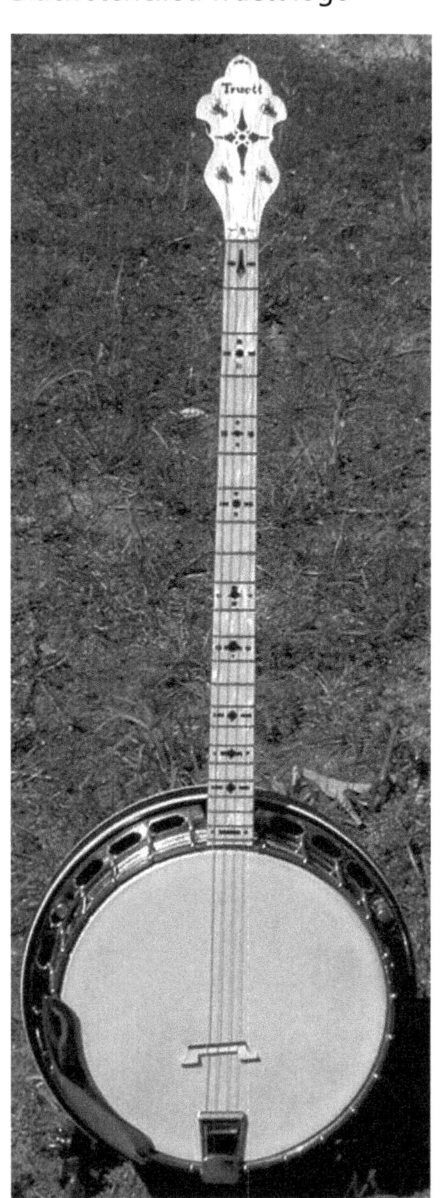

Photos courtesy of Turtlehill Banjos

Other Brands Made By Gibson

Grinnell - 1936

Headquartered in Detroit, Grinnell Brothers was the largest music retailer in Michigan with stores in just about every city in the state. They started as Gibson distributor in the 1920's, but it wasn't until 1936, that they had Gibson manufacture a "Grinnell" branded guitar. This was due in part to several "house-brands" they carried, some of which were made by other companies like C.F. Martin & Co. (Gibson's biggest competitor). There are a few surviving examples of three different Grinnell model guitars, including versions of the Kalamazoo KG-14 and KHG-14, which were referred to as the "Special Spanish" and "Special Hawaiian" models respectively. The Special Spanish being a standard Gibson-made Kalamazoo KG-14 with a 14-fret neck and the name Grinnell stenciled on the headstock. The Special Hawaiian was a re-labeled version of the Kalamazoo KHG (Kalamazoo Hawaiian Guitar) model 14 that had a slightly wider 12-fret neck for Hawaiian lap-style playing. There was also a "Special KG-21" archtop model, named after the Kalamazoo KG-21, a smaller archtop acoustic guitar that was a very popular model.

Guitar Models:
Special Hawaiian flattop guitar
(Pictured right)
Same as Kalamazoo KHG-14

Special Spanish flattop guitar
(Not shown)
Same as Kalamazoo KG-14

Special KG-21 archtop guitar
(Not shown)
Same as Kalamazoo KG-21

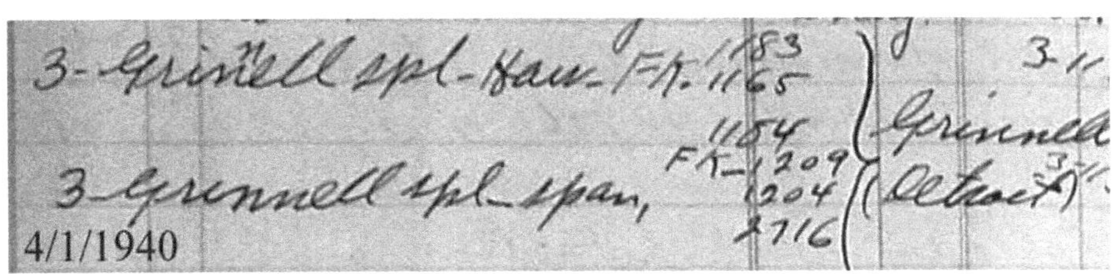
3-Grinnell spl-Haw-F.K. 1183 1165 1184 Grinnell Detroit
3-Grinnell spl-span, FK-1209 1204 1716
4/1/1940

Photos courtesy of Deke Dickerson

Other Brands Made By Gibson

Hayden - 1936

L.D. Heater was a music retailer & wholesaler with locations in Seattle, WA and Portland, OR. It is still unclear how many guitars were sold by L.D. Heater as "Cromwell" and how many were re-labeled as the Hayden brand. There are few surviving examples of this brand, so for the purposes of this book, only the Model G-2 is listed and pictured below. Since there are few surviving examples and no known copies of L.D. Heater catalogs from this era, use the chapter on Cromwell as a reference for the different models listed below.

Flattop Guitar Model:
Re-labeled Cromwell G-2
Body size: 14 ¾" x 19 ¼" (same as KG-14, G-2)
Slightly narrower scalloped peghead design
"skunk stripe" down center of the FB
Stenciled Hayden logo

B&S Barrington - 1939-1940

The B&S Barrington brand was linked to one of Gibson's UK distributors Beare and Sons. The name comes Beare & Sons (B&S) and Richard "Barrington" Beare who joined the long-established family business in 1931. There is only one known instrument Gibson made for B&S, a lap-steel guitar similar to the Kalamazoo KEH. There were other guitars built with the B&S Barrington brand made by Arthur Hensel, but they had no relationship with Gibson.

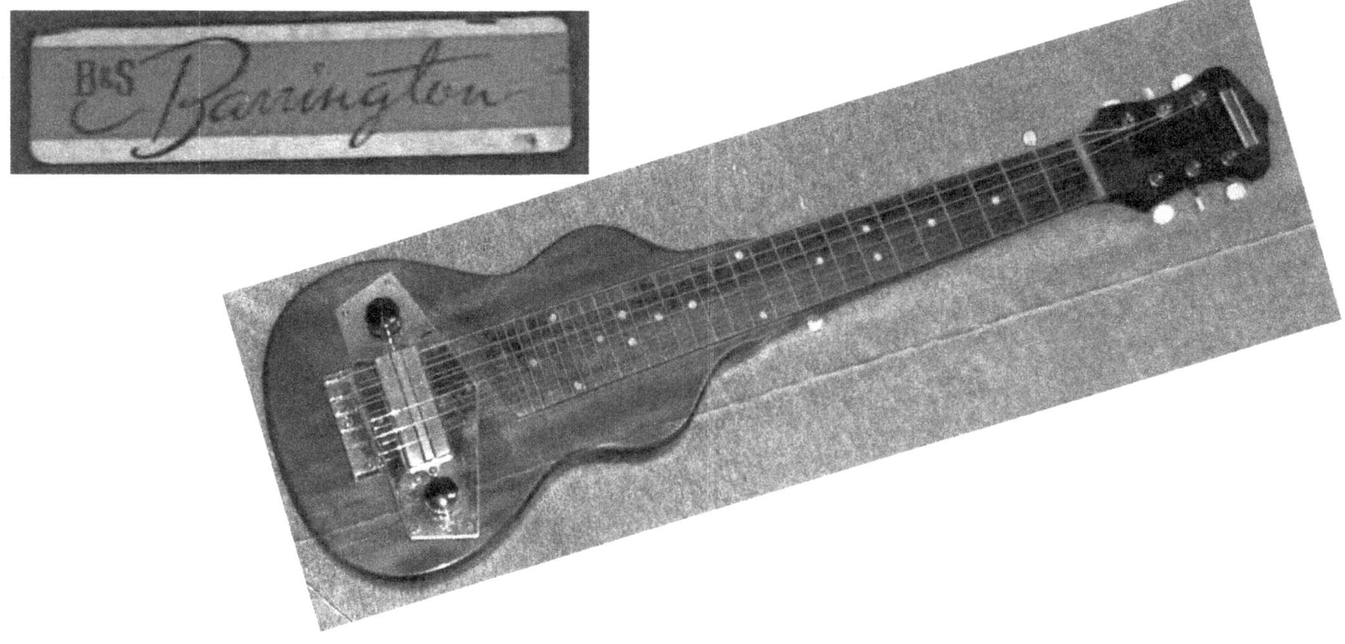

Other Brands Made By Gibson

Oriole - c1926 to 1929

Technically, the Oriole brand was the first "budget brand" Gibson ever produced dating to around 1926-1929, but there's just not a lot of information on this early budget banjo. A brief mention of the Oriole banjo appeared in a J.W. Jenkins distributor catalog for $27.50, which was even less expensive than Gibson's entry-level TB-0 tenor banjo, which cost $35.00. The Oriole brand was used later on certain models of the Kalamazoo line, but apparently had nothing to do with the original use of this name.

Oriole Tenor Banjo:
Small 10 ½" rim
Metal resonator
23" scale length
Ivoroid bound "ebonized" fingerboard
24 nickel brackets
Oriole with fleur-de-lis stencil on peghead

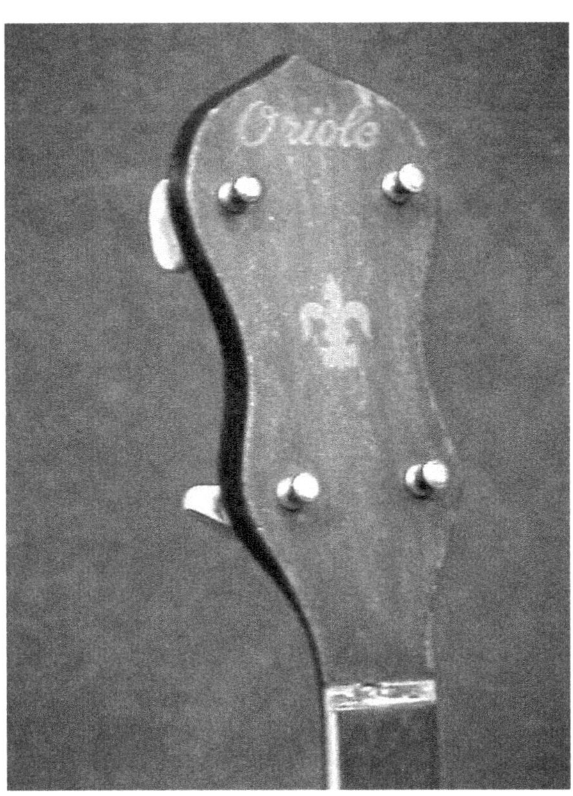

Photos courtesy of Elderly Instruments

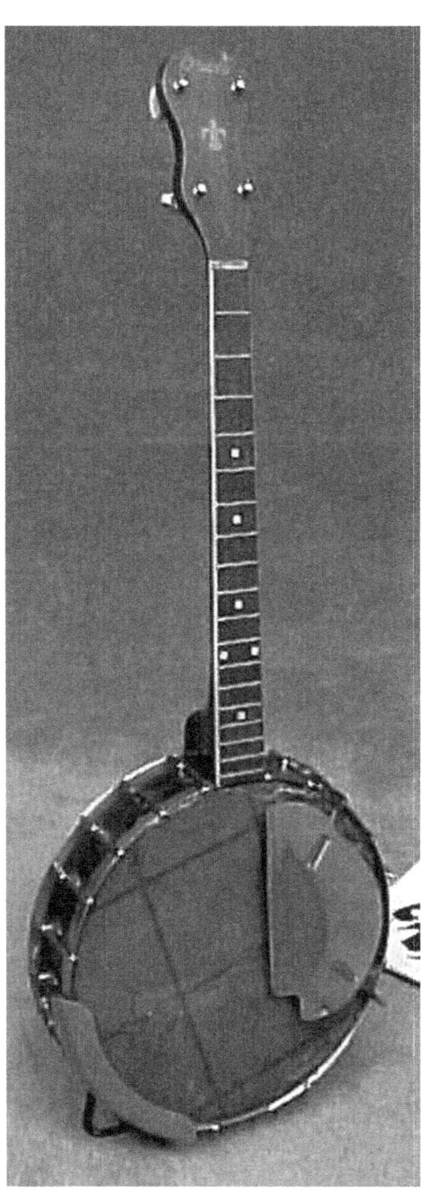

Other Brands Made By Gibson

Liberty - date unknown

Other sources indicate that Gibson made this obscure brand, but there are no known examples and no shipping records that confirm a model called Liberty. It is believed that there was one guitar model, similar to the Kalamazoo KG-11, but this is unconfirmed information.

Paynes for Music - 1937

Like the Liberty brand, other sources indicate that Gibson made a private-label house brand for this Greenville, South Carolina retailer. Unfortunately, there are no known examples, and Gibson shipping records show no "special" type or model guitar being shipped to Paynes, so the information remains unconfirmed.

Other Brands Made By Gibson

Reznick Radio Special - 1936 -1940

Another obscure brand made by Gibson for Reznick Music in Winston-Salem, North Carolina. Called the "Reznick Radio Special", it was an all mahogany Hawaiian guitar similar to the Mastertone Special, and is listed in Gibson's shipping records as "MHG Spl.", which presumably means mahogany Hawaiian guitar special.

Guitar Model:

MHG Special or Reznick Radio Special
Same body as Kalamazoo KHG-11
All mahogany - top, back, sides & neck
3-on-plate tuners with black buttons
12-fret neck
RW fingerboard w/ MOP dots up to 19th fret
Large rectangle bridge - looks like a radio

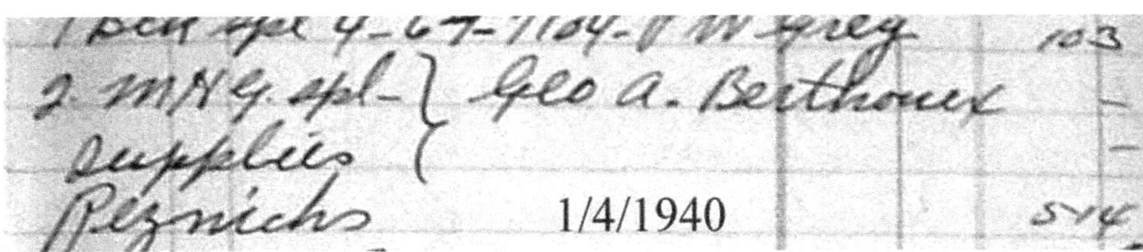

Other Brands Made By Gibson

Tex Star - San Antonio Music - 1936

San Antonio Music was one of the oldest musical merchandise retailers in Texas, established in 1891 by Issac Bledsoe. The San Antonio Music Co. was located at 316 W. Commerce from the 1920s until it closed around 1956. City directories provided a list of the following items sold at the store: "pianos, player pianos, grands, sheet music, radios, records, band and orchestra instruments, washing & sewing machines, vacuum cleaners and every musical instrument." Although no known examples of the "Tex Star" brand exist, Gibson's shipping records indicate that in May 1936, Gibson shipped one "Tex Star" sample guitar, which appears to have been similar to the Kalamazoo model KG-11. San Antonio Music only ordered an additional 12 guitars making them very rare if in fact any of them still exist. It was not out of the ordinary for Gibson to offer dealers such as San Antonio music the opportunity of having a "house brand" usually only requiring an order of a dozen or so of the same model guitar. The same would apply to most of the more obscure brands in this chapter.

Other Brands Made By Gibson

Werlein Leader - 1941

Philip Werlein, Ltd. can date its roots back to the mid-1800's. It was founded by Philip Peter Werlein, a German-born educator and music publisher. Originally settling in Vicksburg, Mississippi, Werlein opened his first music store in 1842. In 1853, he decided to move to a larger city venturing forth to New Orleans. It was after the Civil War that Phillip Werlein, Jr. opened what was called "the largest music store in the South," and located at 731 Canal Street, New Orleans, LA. Unfortunately the original store was destroyed in a fire in 1887, but Werlein's new store at 605 Canal Street would be its new home for nearly 90 years to follow.

Werlein's was already an established Gibson dealer when they had Gibson make "The Werlein Special" so named in the original Gibson shipping ledger entry from March 1941. Werleins only ordered one unit presumably a "sample" and subsequently another 10 matching guitar and amplifier sets a month later. Although no surviving examples are known to exist, it is certain that the "Werlein Special" was virtually the same as the Kalamazoo KEH lap-steel guitar and the amplifier, a Kalamazoo model KEA, as the FONs (factory order numbers) were batches of the very same instruments.

Gibson-made Amplifiers

Gibson made several different varieties of amps either as "in-house" brands like Kalamazoo, Cromwell, and Mastertone, or as "contract" brands such as the amps made for the Montgomery Ward and Spiegel catalogs. All were similar in design to their Gibson counterparts including the components that were assembled at Gibson's Kalamazoo, Michigan factory; Lyon & Healey chassis, Geib cabinets, RCA tubes and either Utah or Jensen speakers. Only the Kalamazoo and Mastertone amps actually had the brand name on them, but all had an unmistakable resemblance to the Gibson amps in particular the Model EH-100 that Gibson first introduced in 1936. Most have the same round black perforated metal speaker grille and were covered in a thick cloth coated in nitro-cellulose lacquer called Keratol, usually embossed to look like leather or imprinted to look like a luggage linen material. Most had one or two instrument inputs with no volume control, plus a high-gain microphone input with volume control. Typically, most amps were sold only as a set with an accompanying instrument with the same model number.

Amplifier Models:

Cromwell EG amp - 1937-1939
(Pictured on page 17)
Dark brown cover & horizontal yellow stripes
Detachable back
10" speaker & 6 tubes

Kalamazoo KEA/KEH - 1937-1939
(Pictured on page 29)
Simulated luggage linen material
Black cover & orange vertical stripes
Kalamazoo logo above speaker grille
8" speaker & 5 tubes

Kalamazoo KEH-R - 1940
(Pitured on page 29)
Detachable upper speaker section
Dark brown covering
10" speaker & 5 tunbes

Mastertone Special - 1939-1942
(pictured on page 41)
Brown covering
Logo stenciled on speaker grille
8" speak & 3 tubes

Gibson-made Amplifiers

Montgomery Ward 1270/1271 - 1937
(Pictured on page 46)
Dark brown faux leather covering
10" speaker & 5 tubes

Montgomery Ward 1128/1129 - 1937-1938
(Pictured on page 46)
Black cover & vertical gray stripes
10" speaker & 5 tubes

Montgomery Ward 1107/1109 - 1937
(Pictured on page 45)
Sold as 'Model A', but same as 1128/1129

Montgomery Ward 1149 Roy Smeck - 1938
(Pictured on page 50)
Similar to Model 1128/1129
10" speaker & 6 tubes

Montgomery Ward 1143 - 1938
Roy Smeck Pro Amp
(Similar to Gibson EH-150)
Black covering with vertical gray stripes
12" speaker & 6 tubes
(Never appeared in Ward's catalog)

Montgomery Ward 1139/1140 - 1938
(Pictured on page 50)
Grenn/gray cloth covering
Square fabric-covered speaker grille
8" speaker & 5 tubes

Montgomery Ward 1001 Model D - 1937
(Pictured on page 46)
Dark brown faux leather covering
10" speaker & 5 tubes

Montgomery Ward 1013 Roy Smeck - 1938-1940
(Pictured on page 46)
Brown luggage linen covering &
Cream horizontal stripes
10" speaker & 6 tubes
7th tube added 1940

Spiegel 8709/8710 - 1937
(Pictured on page 69)
Same as Ward's 1270/1271

Capital EJ Amp - 1937-1938
(Not shown)
Same as Cromwell EG amp
Some with Capital logo in yellow

Werlein Leader - 1941-1942
(Not shown)
Same as Kalamazoo KEH-R

c1938 Montgomery Ward Roy Smeck Pro amplifier

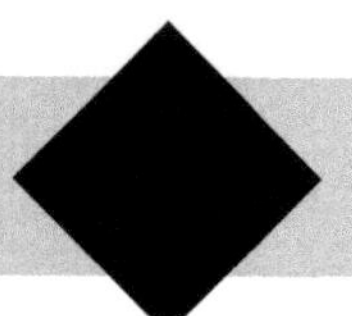

Company	Brand	Model	Type	Approx. Years Mfg.	Approx. Shipping Total	Page #
Beare & Sons	B&S Barrrington	unknown	Lap steel	1937	unknown	84
Buegeleisen & Jacobson	S.S. Stewart	S.S. Stewart	Flattop guitar	1931-1932	unknown	71
Buegeleisen & Jacobson	S.S. Stewart	S.S. Stewart	Tenor banjo	1931-1932	unknown	71
Coast Wholesale	Henry L. Mason	CW-2	Flattop guitar	1936-1939	110	12
Coast Wholesale	Henry L. Mason	CW-4	Archtop guitar	1936-1939	250	12
Coast Wholesale	Henry L. Mason	CW-5	Archtop guitar	1936-1939	25	12
Coast Wholesale	Henry L. Mason	CW-6	Archtop guitar	1936-1939	30	12
Coast Wholesale	Henry L. Mason	CWM-2	Mandolin	1937-1938	23	12
Coast Wholesale	Henry L. Mason	CWM-4	Mandolin	1937-1938	13	12
Coast Wholesale	Henry L. Mason	CW-M5	Mandolin	1936	1	12
Coast Wholesale	Henry L. Mason	CW-M6	Mandolin	1936	1	12
Coast Wholesale	Henry L. Mason	CWT-2	Tenor guitar	1936-1937	14	12
Coast Wholesale	Henry L. Mason	CWT-4	Tenor guitar	1936-1937	7	12
Francis, Day & Hunter	FDH	FDH Special	Archtop guitar	1937-1940	123	18
Gibson, Inc.	Cromwell	EG Amp	Amp	1937	43	17
Gibson, Inc.	Cromwell	EG-5	Electric guitar	1937	23	17
Gibson, Inc.	Cromwell	EGH	Lap steel	1937	34	17
Gibson, Inc.	Cromwell	G-2	Elec. mandolin	1937	12	15
Gibson, Inc.	Cromwell	G-4	Flattop guitar	1936-1940	270	15
Gibson, Inc.	Cromwell	G-5	Archtop guitar	1936-1940	1882	16
Gibson, Inc.	Cromwell	G-6	Archtop guitar	1936-1940	294	16
Gibson, Inc.	Cromwell	G-8	Archtop guitar	1936-1940	170	16
Gibson, Inc.	Cromwell	GM-2	Mandolin	1936-1940	31	17
Gibson, Inc.	Cromwell	GM-4	Mandolin	1936-1940	129	17
Gibson, Inc.	Cromwell	GM-5	Mandolin	1936-1937	19	N/A
Gibson, Inc.	Cromwell	GM-6	Mandolin	1936-1937	9	N/A
Gibson, Inc.	Cromwell	GT-2	Tenor guitar	1936-1937	11	16
Gibson, Inc.	Cromwell	GT-4	Tenor guitar	1936-1940	68	16
Gibson, Inc.	Kalamazoo	KEA	Amp	1938-1941	1392	29
Gibson, Inc.	Kalamazoo	KEA-R	Amp	1940	180	29
Gibson, Inc.	Kalamazoo	KEH	Lap steel	1938-1940	986	29
Gibson, Inc.	Kalamazoo	KEH	Lap steel	1939-1941	49	29
Gibson, Inc.	Kalamazoo	KEH	7-string steel	1940	10	29
Gibson, Inc.	Kalamazoo	KEHC	Lap steel	1939	24	N/A
Gibson, Inc.	Kalamazoo	KEHR Oriole	Lap steel	1940-1941	222	29
Gibson, Inc.	Kalamazoo	KES	Electric guitar	1939-1940	169	28
Gibson, Inc.	Kalamazoo	KESR Oriole	Electric guitar	1940	32	N/A
Gibson, Inc.	Kalamazoo	KES-TG Elec.	Tenor guitar	1940	1	N/A
Gibson, Inc.	Kalamazoo	KG Sport	Flattop guitar	1936-1941	1148	24
Gibson, Inc.	Kalamazoo	KG-11	Flattop guitar	1933-1942	5209	21
Gibson, Inc.	Kalamazoo	KG-14	Flattop guitar	1936-1942	3405	23
Gibson, Inc.	Kalamazoo	KG-16	Archtop guitar	1939-1941	1586	22

Company	Brand	Model	Type	Approx. Years Mfg.	Approx. Shipping Total	Page #
Gibson, Inc.	Kalamazoo	KG-21	Archtop guitar	1934-1941	2677	25
Gibson, Inc.	Kalamazoo	KG-31	Archtop guitar	1934-1941	1717	25
Gibson, Inc.	Kalamazoo	KG-32	Archtop guitar	1939-1941	588	26
Gibson, Inc.	Kalamazoo	KGN-12	Flattop guitar	1939-1940	1708	23
Gibson, Inc.	Kalamazoo	KGN-32	Archtop guitar	1940-1941	582	27
Gibson, Inc.	Kalamazoo	KH-21	Mandola	1936-1939	52	30
Gibson, Inc.	Kalamazoo	KH-22	Mandola	1939	4	31
Gibson, Inc.	Kalamazoo	KHG-11	Hawaiian guitar	1934-1940	983	21
Gibson, Inc.	Kalamazoo	KHG-12	Hawaiian guitar	1939-1941	35	N/A
Gibson, Inc.	Kalamazoo	KHG-14	Hawaiian guitar	1936-1941	740	24
Gibson, Inc.	Kalamazoo	KHGN-12	Hawaiian guitar	1940-1941	75	N/A
Gibson, Inc.	Kalamazoo	KJ	Mando-bass	1937-1939	1939	31
Gibson, Inc.	Kalamazoo	KK-31	Mando-cello	1936-1940	35	30
Gibson, Inc.	Kalamazoo	KK-32	Mando-cello	1940	2	31
Gibson, Inc.	Kalamazoo	KM-11	Mandolin	1933-1941	1154	32
Gibson, Inc.	Kalamazoo	KM-12	Mandolin	1939-1941	942	32
Gibson, Inc.	Kalamazoo	KM-21	Mandolin	1936-1940	603	32
Gibson, Inc.	Kalamazoo	KM-22	Mandolin	1939-1941	237	32
Gibson, Inc.	Kalamazoo	KMB	Mandolin banjo	1935-1941	96	33
Gibson, Inc.	Kalamazoo	KMN-12	Mandolin	1940-1941	816	33
Gibson, Inc.	Kalamazoo	KPB	Plectrum banjo	1933-1941	35	33
Gibson, Inc.	Kalamazoo	KRB	5-string banjp	1933-1941	474	33
Gibson, Inc.	Kalamazoo	KTB	Tenor banjo	1933-1941	403	33
Gibson, Inc.	Kalamazoo	KTG-11	Tenor guitar	1933-1941	105	N/A
Gibson, Inc.	Kalamazoo	KTG-12	Tenor guitar	1939-1941	45	N/A
Gibson, Inc.	Kalamazoo	KTG-14	Tenor guitar	1936-1941	204	N/A
Gibson, Inc.	Kalamazoo	KTG-21	Tenor guitar	1933-1941	117	N/A
Gibson, Inc.	Kalamazoo	KTG-31	Tenor guitar	1933-1941	32	N/A
Gibson, Inc.	Kalamazoo	KTGN-12	Tenor guitar	1940-1941	67	N/A
Gibson, Inc.	Kalamazoo	MEA	Amp	1940-1941	679	N/A
Gibson, Inc.	Kel Kroydon	KK-1	Flatttop guitar	1930-1932	unknown	35
Gibson, Inc.	Kel Kroydon	KK-2	Tenor banjo	1930-1932	unknown	35
Gibson, Inc.	Kel Kroydon	KK-10	Tenor banjo	1930-1932	unknown	36
Gibson, Inc.	Kel Kroydon	KK-11	Flatttop guitar	1930-1932	unknown	36
Gibson, Inc.	Kel Kroydon	KK-20	Mandolin	1930-1932	unknown	37
Gibson, Inc.	Kel Kroydon	KK-21	Mandolin	1930-1932	unknown	37
Gibson, Inc.	Mastertone Special	ME-HAW	Electric guitar	1937-1941	554	41
Gibson, Inc.	Mastertone Special	ME-SP	Electric guitar	1937-1941	157	41
Gibson, Inc.	Mastertone Special	MSG	Flattop guitar	1937-1941	3199	41
Gibson, Inc.	Mastertone Special	MSH	Lap steel guitar	1937-1941	2000	41
Gibson, Inc.	Oriole	unknown	Tenor banjo	1929-1930	unknown	85

Company	Brand	Model	Type	Approx. Years Mfg.	Approx. Shipping Total	Page #
Gretsch & Brenner	Ambassador	C-5	unknown	1936	10	9
Gretsch & Brenner	Ambassador	C-7	unknown	1936	10	9
Gretsch & Brenner	Ambassador	M-11	Archtop guitar	1936	5	9
Gretsch & Brenner	Ambassador	M-5	Archtop guitar	1936	18	9
Gretsch & Brenner	Ambassador	M-7	Archtop guitar	1936	6	9
Gretsch & Brenner	Ambassador	M-9	Archtop guitar	1936	27	9
Grinnell Brothers	Grinnell	KG-21	Archtop guitar	1936-1937	6	83
Grinnell Brothers	Grinnell	Special Haw.	Flattop guitar	1936-1937	35	83
Grinnell Brothers	Grinnell	Special Span.	Flattop guitar	1936-1937	unknown	83
J.W. Jenkins	Capital	EG amp	Amp	1937	7	11
J.W. Jenkins	Capital	EGH	Lap steel guitar	1937	6	11
J.W. Jenkins	Capital	EJ-3	Electric guitar	1937	2	11
J.W. Jenkins	Capital	EJ-5	Electric guitar	1937	1	11
J.W. Jenkins	Capital	EJM	Elec. mandolin	1937	1	11
J.W. Jenkins	Capital	J-1/J-15	Flattop guitar	1937-1938	75	11
J.W. Jenkins	Capital	J-2 Tenor	Tenor guitar	1936-1938	unknown	11
J.W. Jenkins	Capital	J-2/J-16	Archtop guitar	1936-1937	140	11
J.W. Jenkins	Capital	J-3/J-17	Archtop guitar	1937-1938	53	11
J.W. Jenkins	Capital	JM-2/JM-4	Mandolin	1937-1938	12	11
Kalamazoo Musical Inst.	Martelle	Deluxe	Flattop Jumbo	1934	unknown	40
Kalamazoo Musical Inst.	Martelle	Deluxe Custom	Flattop Jumbo	1934	unknown	40
L.D. Heater Music	Hayden	G-2	Flattop guitar	1937-1939	unknown	84
L.D. Heater Music	Hayden	G-4	Archtop guitar	1937-1939	unknown	84
L.D. Heater Music	Hayden	G-6	Archtop guitar	1937-1939	unknown	84
Lilian G. Marshall	Marshall Special	Marshall Special	Flattop guitar	1930	unknown	39
Montgomery Ward	Andy Sanella	682	Flattop guitar	1934-1935	unknown	44
Montgomery Ward	Carson Robison	926	Flattop guitar	1933-1936	unknown	45
Montgomery Ward	Carson Robison	1052	Flattop guitar	1939-1940	738	48
Montgomery Ward	Carson Robison	1115	Flattop guitar	1936-1939	1903	48
Montgomery Ward	Carson Robison	1134	Flattop guitar	1937-1940	447	N/A
Montgomery Ward	Carson Robison	1135	3/4 size guitar	1936-1940	148	48
Montgomery Ward	Carson Robison	1281	Flattop guitar	1936-1937	345	48
Montgomery Ward	Charles McNeil	1593	Tenor Banjo	1937-1939	240	54
Montgomery Ward	Mitchell Bros	732	Tenor Banjo	1934-1935	unknown	54
Montgomery Ward	Mitchell Bros	1584	5-string banjo	1934-1936	110	54
Montgomery Ward	None	952	Tenor Banjo	1940	61	56
Montgomery Ward	None	953	5-string banjo	1940	76	56
Montgomery Ward	None	954	Tenor Banjo	1940	81	56
Montgomery Ward	None	955	5-string banjo	1940	87	56
Montgomery Ward	None	956	Tenor Banjo	1940	57	56
Montgomery Ward	None	957	5-string banjo	1940	22	56
Montgomery Ward	None	969	Mandolin	1940	192	56

Company	Brand	Model	Type	Approx. Years Mfg.	Approx. Shipping Total	Page #
Montgomery Ward	Recording King	505	Tenor Banjo	1930-1931	unknown	53
Montgomery Ward	Recording King	507	Tenor Banjo	1930-1931	unknown	42
Montgomery Ward	Recording King	681	Archtop guitar	1930-1931	unknown	44
Montgomery Ward	Recording King	701	Tenor Banjo	1930-1931	unknown	55
Montgomery Ward	Recording King	774	Tenor Banjo	1931-1932	unknown	N/A
Montgomery Ward	Recording King	803	Tenor Banjo	1933-1934	unknown	N/A
Montgomery Ward	Recording King	807	Flattop guitar	1930-1931	unknown	42
Montgomery Ward	Recording King	807	Mandolin	1934-1936	unknown	57
Montgomery Ward	Recording King	811	Flattop guitar	1931-1932	unknown	45
Montgomery Ward	Recording King	853	Archtop guitar	1933-1935	unknown	45
Montgomery Ward	Recording King	1005	Model D steel	1938-1939	83	46
Montgomery Ward	Recording King	1007	Model A set	1938-1939	14	46
Montgomery Ward	Recording King	1008	Amp	1936-1938	unknown	46
Montgomery Ward	Recording King	1009	Amp	1936-1938	unknown	46
Montgomery Ward	Recording King	1010	Model A ES	1937-1938	unknown	N/A
Montgomery Ward	Recording King	1015	Archtop guitar	1939-1940	229	N/A
Montgomery Ward	Recording King	1020	Model A Steel	1939	89	46
Montgomery Ward	Recording King	1022	Amp	1936-1938	unknown	46
Montgomery Ward	Ray Whitley	1027	Jumbo guitar	1937-1938	153	47
Montgomery Ward	Ray Whitley	1028	Jumbo guitar	1938-1939	191	47
Montgomery Ward	Recording King	1101	Archtop guitar	1940	155	N/A
Montgomery Ward	Recording King	1103	M-3 guitar	1940	117	49
Montgomery Ward	Recording King	1121	17" M-5 nickel	1939-1940	102	52
Montgomery Ward	Recording King	1122	17" M-5 gold	1939-1940	68	52
Montgomery Ward	Recording King	1123	M-4 guitar	1938-1939	372	49
Montgomery Ward	Recording King	1124	16" M-5	1937-1939	421	49
Montgomery Ward	Recording King	1127	A-104 Smeck	1939-1940	180	46
Montgomery Ward	Recording King	1128	A-104 Smeck	1938	20	46
Montgomery Ward	Recording King	1128	Elec. Span. Set	1937-1938	146	46
Montgomery Ward	Recording King	1129	Elec. Haw. Set	1937-1938	23	50
Montgomery Ward	Recording King	1129	Smeck Amps	1937-1938	118	50
Montgomery Ward	Recording King	1136	M-2 guitar	1938-1939	740	49
Montgomery Ward	Recording King	1137	M-3 guitar	1938-1939	562	49
Montgomery Ward	Recording King	1139	Model A set	1938	10	50
Montgomery Ward	Recording King	1140	Model A Span.	1938	37	N/A
Montgomery Ward	Recording King	1149	Smeck Amps	1938	unknown	91
Montgomery Ward	Recording King	1151	AB-104	1939	2	50
Montgomery Ward	Recording King	1171	M-5 guitar	1938-1939	40	49
Montgomery Ward	Recording King	1284	Archtop guitar	1936-1937	unknown	51
Montgomery Ward	Recording King	1285	Archtop guitar	1936-1937	140	51
Montgomery Ward	Recording King	1607	Mandolin	1935-1936	11	57
Montgomery Ward	Recording King	1642	Mandolin	1936-1937	129	57

Company	Brand	Model	Type	Approx. Years Mfg.	Approx. Shipping Total	Page #
Montgomery Ward	Roy Smeck	1013	Smeck Amp	1938-1939	16	46
Montgomery Ward	Roy Smeck	1022	AB-104 Smeck	1939	41	46
Montgomery Ward	Roy Smeck	1023	AB-104 Steel	1939	205	46
Montgomery Ward	Roy Smeck	1025	8-string console	1939-1940	13	52
Montgomery Ward	Roy Smeck	1140	Pro Haw. Set	1938	2	50
Montgomery Ward	Roy Smeck	1142	Pro Haw.	1938	2	46
Montgomery Ward	Roy Smeck	1143	Pro Amp	1938	24	46
Montgomery Ward	Roy Smeck	1144	Pro Spanish	1938	5	N/A
Montgomery Ward	Roy Smeck	1145	Pro Spanish	1938	2	N/A
Montgomery Ward	Studio King	605	Tenor Banjo	1930-1931	unknown	55
Montgomery Ward	Studio King	641	Tenor Banjo	1929-1930	unknown	53
Montgomery Ward	Studio King	645	Tenor Banjo	1929-1930	unknown	53
Montgomery Ward	Tone Crest	1282	Archtop guitar	1936-1937	unknown	51
Montgomery Ward	Tone Crest	1283	Archtop guitar	1936-1937	unknown	51
Montgomery Ward	Wards	731	Tenor Banjo	1934-1935	unknown	54
Montgomery Ward	Wards	1586	Tenor banjo	1935-1936	unknown	N/A
National/Valco Mfg.	National	510-4	unknown	1944-1946	5	N/A
National/Valco Mfg.	National	B-125	unknown	1944-1946	2	59
National/Valco Mfg.	National	Gibson Spl	unknown	1944-1946	2	N/A
National/Valco Mfg.	National	N.S.	Jumbo guitar	1944-1946	2	59
National/Valco Mfg.	National	N-100	Jumbo guitar	1944-1946	7	59
National/Valco Mfg.	National	N-111	Jumbo guitar	1944-1946	4	61
National/Valco Mfg.	National	N-12	Archtop guitar	1944-1946	2	59
National/Valco Mfg.	National	N-125	Archtop guitar	1944-1946	1	59
National/Valco Mfg.	National	N-150	Archtop guitar	1944-1946	2	59
National/Valco Mfg.	National	N-275	Archtop guitar	1944-1946	5	61
National/Valco Mfg.	National	N-31	Mandolin	1944-1946	4	59
National/Valco Mfg.	National	N-33	Flattop guitar	1944-1946	2	59
National/Valco Mfg.	National	N-4	Archtop guitar	1944-1946	2	59
National/Valco Mfg.	National	N-45	Jumbo guitar	1944-1946	2	59
National/Valco Mfg.	National	N-5 N	Archtop guitar	1944-1946	1	59
National/Valco Mfg.	National	N-5 R	Archtop guitar	1944-1946	1	59
National/Valco Mfg.	National	N-50	Archtop guitar	1944-1946	2	59
National/Valco Mfg.	National	N-66	Jumbo guitar	1944-1946	4	59
National/Valco Mfg.	National	N-7	Archtop guitar	1944-1946	3	59
National/Valco Mfg.	National	NE-125	Electric guitar	1944	2	59
National/Valco Mfg.	National	NE-150	Electric guitar	1944	2	59
National/Valco Mfg.	National	NE-300	Electric guitar	1944	2	59
National/Valco Mfg.	National	NM-00	Mandolin	1944	1	59
National/Valco Mfg.	National	NM-50	Mandolin	1944	2	59
National/Valco Mfg.	National	N-So.	Jumbo guitar	1944-1946	4	59

Company	Brand	Model	Type	Approx. Years Mfg.	Approx. Shipping Total	Page #
National/Valco Mfg.	National	1135	Archtop guitar	1948-1952	unknown	62
National/Valco Mfg.	National	1145	Archtop guitar	1948-1952	unknown	62
National/Valco Mfg.	National	1155	Flattop guitar	1948-1961	unknown	63
National/Valco Mfg.	National	1155E	Acoustic elec.	1948-1961	unknown	63
National/Valco Mfg.	National	1160	Flattop guitar	1948-1952	unknown	64
National/Valco Mfg.	National	1110	Aristocrat elec.	1948-1952	unknown	64
National/Valco Mfg.	National	1109	Bel-Aire elec.	1954-1961	unknown	65
National/Valco Mfg.	National	1198E	Bel-Aire elec.	1954-1961	unknown	65
National/Valco Mfg.	National	1103	Del-Mar elec.	1954-1961	unknown	66
Paynes For Music	Paynes	N/A	unknown	unknown	unknown	86
Philip Werlein	Werlein Leader	Werlein Leader	Amp	1941	10	89
Philip Werlein	Werlein Leader	Werlein Leader	Electric guitar	1941	11	89
Reznick's Music	Reznick Radio Special	N/A	Flatttop guitar	1937	unknown	87
San Antonio Music	Tex Star	KG Special	Flattop guitar	1936	13	88
Spiegel, May, Stern	Old Kraftsman	2154	Archtop guitar	1936	205	70
Spiegel, May, Stern	Old Kraftsman	8707	Archtop guitar	1937	56	69
Spiegel, May, Stern	Old Kraftsman	8708	Archtop guitar	1937	48	69
Spiegel, May, Stern	Old Kraftsman	8709	Electric guitar	1937	67	69
Spiegel, May, Stern	Old Kraftsman	8710	Hawaiian steel	1937	43	69
Tonk Brothers	Fascinator	4960	Flattop guitar	1935-1936	unknown	72
Tonk Brothers	Fascinator	4970	Archtop guitar	1935-1936	unknown	74
Tonk Brothers	Fascinator	4980	Archtop guitar	1935-1936	unknown	73
Tonk Brothers	Fascinator	5284	Mandolin	1935-1936	unknown	74
Tonk Brothers	Washburn	5240	Flattop guitar	1938-1940	95	76
Tonk Brothers	Washburn	5241	Flattop guitar	1939-1940	19	76
Tonk Brothers	Washburn	5242	Archtop guitar	1938-1940	26	77
Tonk Brothers	Washburn	5243	Archtop guitar	1939	26	77
Tonk Brothers	Washburn	5244	Flattop guitar	1938-1940	39	78
Tonk Brothers	Washburn	5246	Flattop guitar	1938-1940	35	78
Tonk Brothers	Washburn	5248	Archtop guitar	1939	15	79
Tonk Brothers	Washburn	5249	Flattop guitar	1938-1940	41	79
Tonk Brothers	Washburn	5280	Mandolin	1938-1939	12	80
Tonk Brothers	Washburn	5281	Mandolin	1938-1939	12	80
Trujo Banjo Company	Trujo	unknown	Flattop guitar	1930-1932	unknown	82
Trujo Banjo Company	Truett	Style 1	Tenor banjo	1930-1932	unknown	82
Trujo Banjo Company	Truett	Style 2	Tenor banjo	1930-1932	unknown	82
Unknown	Liberty	unknown	unknown	unknown	unknown	86

Index

About the Author

Paul Fox is a musical instrument researcher and historian with a particular emphasis on the Gibson and Epiphone companies. His article on the "House of Stathopoulo Harp Guitar" was published in the May 2010 issue of Vintage Guitar Magazine. He is also a published author of several bass guitar books, including "How To Play The Bass Guitar" first published in 1978.

His two great passions in life are guitars and woodworking that he has combined to create his own company, Fox Guitars, a life-long dream come true. Fox Guitars is based in the Boston area in Lowell, Massachusetts and is dedicated to building the finest custom hand-made guitars inspired by great vintage guitars of the 1920s and 1930s. His company, www.fox-guitars.com offers both acoustic and electric "new vintage series" guitar models that are completely handcrafted from the finest materials available, including spruce, mahogany, maple, rosewood, and ebony. Each one is carefully constructed, tested, and finely tuned to capture that great 'pre-war' vintage tone, while incorporating many modern improvements and building.

Fox Guitars also offers full guitar repair and restoration services. The Fox Guitars website also includes lots of FREE guitar history, including vintage guitar data about Gibson and Epiphone, including catalogs, old magazines & advertisements, patents, historic information and much more.

More Great Books from Centerstream...

COWBOY GUITARS
by Steve Evans and Ron Middlebrook
foreword by Roy Rogers, Jr.

Back in the good old days, all of America was infatuated with the singing cowboys of movies and radio. This huge interest led to the production of "cowboy guitars." This fun, fact-filled book is an outstanding roundup of these wonderful instruments.

00000281 Softcover (232 pages)....$35.00
00000303 Hardcover (234 pages)....$55.00

SPANN'S GUIDE TO GIBSON
1902-1941
by Joe Spann

This detailed look at the inner workings of the famous musical instrument manufacturer of Kalamazoo, Michigan before World War II. For the first time, Gibson fans can learn about the employees who built the instruments, exactly where the raw materials came from, the identity of parts vendors, and how the production was carried out. The book explains Gibson's per-World War II factory order number (FON) and serial number systems, and corrects long-standing chronological errors. Previously unknown information about every aspect of the operation is covered in-depth. Noted historian Joe Spann gathered firsthand info from per-war employees, and had access to major Gibson collections around the world. Long time Gibson experts, as well as casual collectors, will find this volume an indispensable addition to their reference shelf.

00001525 302 pages....$39.99

THE GIBSON 175
Its History and Its Players
by Adrian Ingram

Debuting in 1949 and in continuous production ever since, the ES-175 is one of the most versatile and famous guitars in music history. The first Gibson electric to feature a Florentine cutaway, the ES-175 was also one of the first Electric Spanish guitars to be fitted with P.A.F. humbuckers and is prized for its playability, craftsmanship, and full rich tone. Written by noted author/guitarist Adrian Ingram, contents include: the complete history of the 175, The Players, a beautiful ES-175 Color Gallery, Chronology, Shipping Totals, and more. This book is a must for every guitar player and enthusiast or collector.

00001134 ....$24.95

THE GIBSON 335
Its History and Its Players
by Adrian Ingram

Gibson's first "semi-acoustic" the ES-335, which was neither totally solid nor fully acoustic, is the guitar of choice used by many famous guitarists such as Andy Summers, Elvin Bishop, Lee Ritenour, Jay Graydon, Robben Ford, Freddie King, John McLaughin, Jimmy Page, Chuck Berry, Tony Mottola, Johnny Rivers, Jack Wilkins, Bono, Grant Green, Eric Clapton, Stevie Ray Vaughan, Alvin Lee, B.B. King, Emily Remler, Otis Rush, Pete Townshend, John Lee Hooker, and Larry Carlton. This book includes the complete history of the 335, the players, a beautiful color section, chronology, shipping totals and more. A must-have for every 335 player and guitar enthusiast or collector!

00000353 120 pages....$29.95

THE GIBSON L5
by Adrian Ingram

Introduced in 1922, the Gibson L5 is the precursor of the modern archtop guitar. This book takes a look at its history and most famous players, from its creation, through the Norlin years, to its standing today as the world's most popular jazz guitar. Includes a 16-page full color photo section.

00000216 112 pages....$29.95

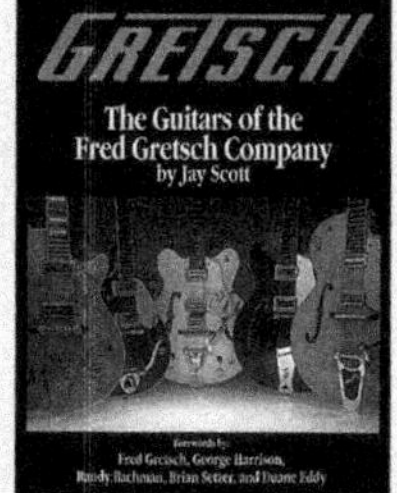

GRETSCH – THE GUITARS OF THE FRED GRETSCH COMPANY
by Jay Scott

This comprehensive manual uncovers the history of Gretsch guitars through 32 pages of color photos, hundreds of black & white photos, and forewords by Fred Gretsch, George Harrison, Randy Bachman, Brian Setzer, and Duane Eddy. It covers each model in depth, including patent numbers and drawings for collectors.

00000142 286 pages....$35.00

THE HISTORY & ARTISTRY OF NATIONAL RESONATOR INSTRUMENTS
by Bob Brozman

This book is a history book, source book and owner's manual for players and fans that covers the facts and figures necessary for serious collectors. In addition to many black and white historical photos, there is a 32-page color section, and appendixes with serial numbers for all instruments, a company chronology, and a Hawaiian Artist Discography.

00000154 296 pages....$35.00

P.O. Box 17878 - Anaheim Hills, CA 92817
(714) 779-9390 www.centerstream-usa.com

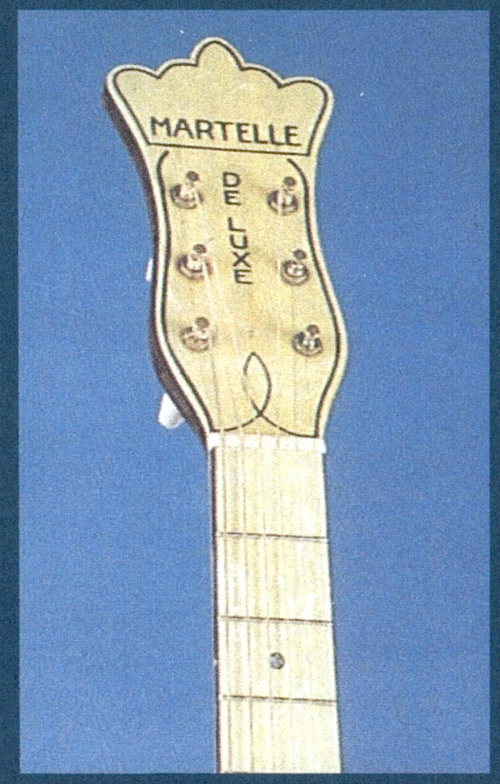

A one of a kind 1934 Martelle Deluxe custom jumbo probably made for Charles Martelle, owner of Kalamazoo Musical Instruments. Owned by Dennis Watkins. *Photo by Dan Loftin. Courtesy of Gruhn Guitars*

The Grinnell model "Special Spanish"
Courtesy of Stan Werbin at Elderly Instruments in Lansing, Michigan, www.elderly.com. Photos by Dave Matchette

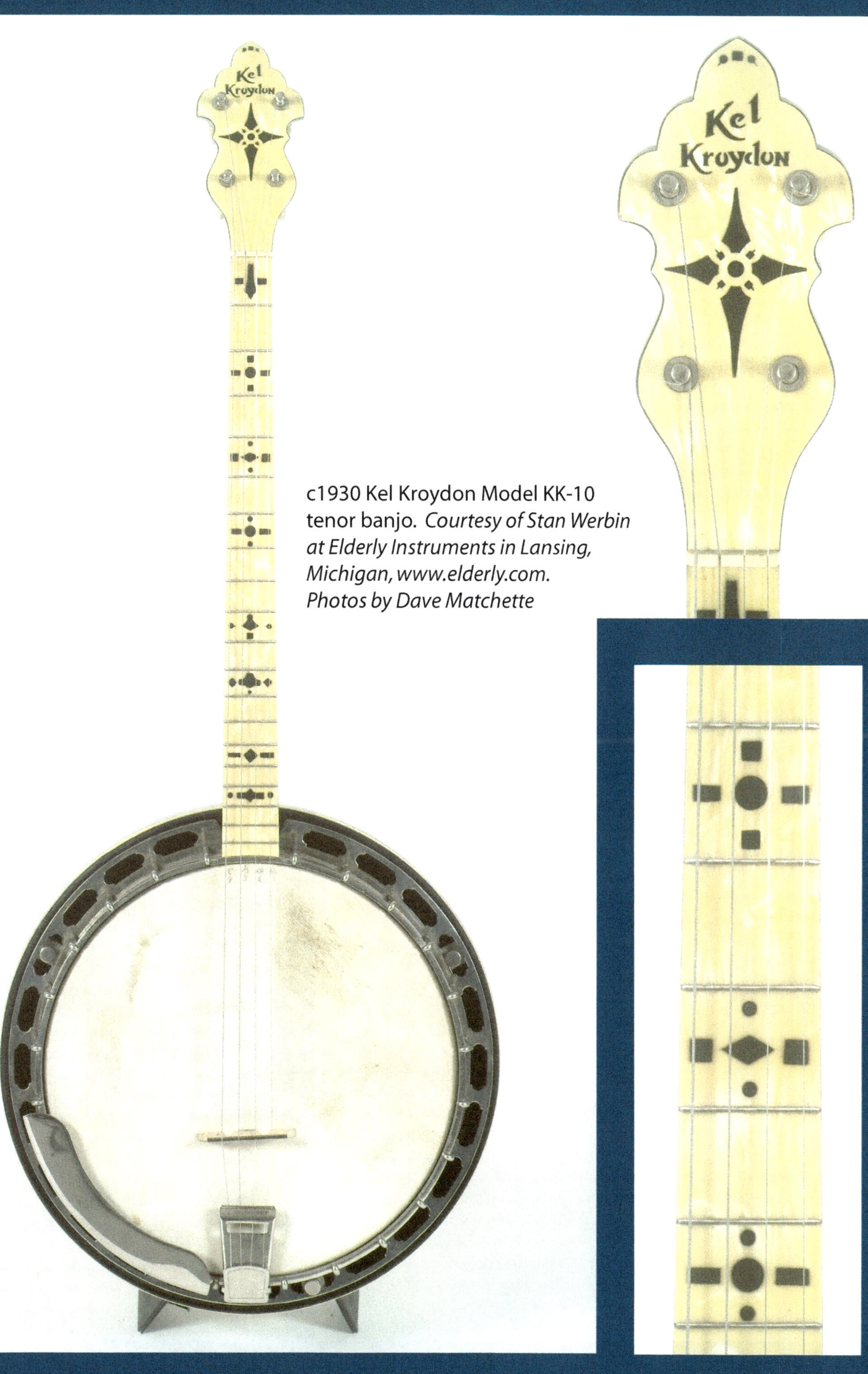

c1930 Kel Kroydon Model KK-10 tenor banjo. *Courtesy of Stan Werbin at Elderly Instruments in Lansing, Michigan, www.elderly.com. Photos by Dave Matchette*

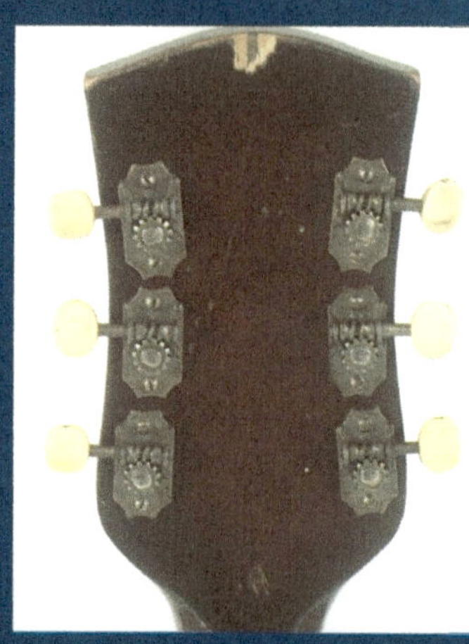

Extremely rare Gibson-made National Model N-111 "prototype" flattop guitar. *Courtesy of Stan Werbin at Elderly Instruments in Lansing, Michigan, www.elderly.com. Photos by Dave Matchette*

1942 Kalamazoo KGN-12.
Courtesy of Folkway Music

The Kalamazoo "Sport" model 3/4-size guitar.
Courtesy of Folkway Music

Recording King Model 1124
archtop acoustic guitar.
*Courtesy of Stan Werbin
at Elderly Instruments in Lansing,
Michigan, www.elderly.com.
Photos by Dave Matchette*

Recording King Model AB-104
Roy Smeck Hawaiian lap steel
Courtesy of Stan Werbin
at Elderly Instruments in Lansing,
Michigan, www.elderly.com.
Photos by Dave Matchette

The elegant top-of-the-line
Recording King Model M-5
Courtesy of Stan Werbin
at Elderly Instruments in Lansing,
Michigan, www.elderly.com.
Photos by Dave Matchette

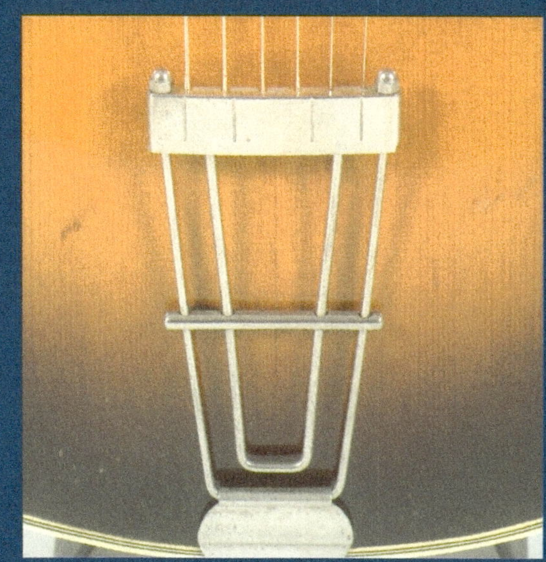

A rare and unusual Gibson-made Trujo tenor banjo with carved "figure head" pegboard. *Courtesy of Stan Werbin at Elderly Instruments in Lansing, Michigan, www.elderly.com. Photos by Dave Matchette*

A 1937 Cromwell model EG-5 electric guitar. Note the backward mounted "Charlie Christian" style pickup. *Photo by Tom Walzem Courtesy of Mike Newton*

A 1937 Cromwell model EG-H lap steel guitar.
Photo by Tom Walzem
Courtesy of Mike Newton

An unusual c1939 Recording King Ray Whitley-style guitar model without the Ray Whitley logo, nicknamed the RK J-55.
Courtesy of Folkway Music

A 1930 Kel Kroydon Model KK-1, retailed for $20.00 vs. $75.00 for a Gibson L-2. *Courtesy of Folkway Music*

A rare example of a mid-1930s Gibson-made Cromwell Model GM-4 mandolin. *Courtesy of Folkway Music*

The Kel Kroydon Model KK-1 with added twin parrot stencil design on the body. *Courtesy of Folkway Music*

1934 Martelle Deluxe originally with wide neck similar to the Gibson Roy Smeck Stage Deluxe.
Courtesy of Folkway Music

A c1934 Montgomery Ward Carson J. Robison model 926, similar to the Kalamazoo KG-11. *Courtesy of Folkway Music*

The Cromwell model G-4 archtop guitar model with signature "skunk stripe" down the fingerboard.
Courtesy of Folkway Music

The Kalamazoo Model KTG-11 tenor guitar never appeared in any brochure or catalog, but was simply a KG-11 with a tenor neck. *Courtesy of Folkway Music*

Recording King Model M-3 archtop guitar. *Courtesy of Folkway Music*

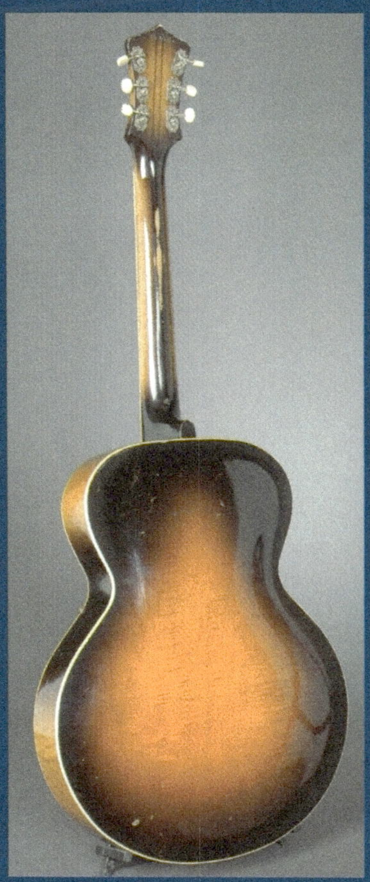

The Kalamazoo model KG-31 archtop guitar. *Courtesy of Folkway Music*

A c1948-1949 National model 1160 flattop guitar Gibson made both the body and the neck and was basically the same as their model LG-3. *Courtesy of Folkway Music*

The extremely rare 1930 Gibson-made Marshall Special flattop guitar similar to the Kel Kroydon model KK-2. *Owned by Neil Reck Courtesy of Tony Klassen*